steam safari

LAST STEAM LOCOMOTIVES OF THE WORLD

steam safari

Written and photographed
by
COLIN GARRATT

LONDON
BLANDFORD PRESS

First published 1974

© 1974 Blandford Press Ltd,
167 High Holborn, London WC1V 6PH

ISBN 0 7137 0712 7

All photographs in this book were taken with a Praktica camera
using 50-mm Tessar and Pancolar lenses and a 135-mm Jena 'S' lens,
on Agfacolor C.T. 18 reversal film.

Colour section printed in 4-colour lithography
by Colour Reproductions Ltd, Billericay.
Text set in 9 on 10 point 'Monophoto' Baskerville
by Keyspools Ltd, Golborne, Lancs
Printed and bound by Tinling (1973) Ltd, London and Prescot

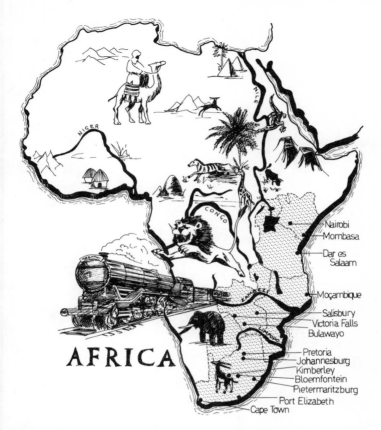

AFRICA

This volume contains a selection of locomotives from the following countries:

Country	Railway company	Gauge
South Africa	South African Railways (S.A.R.)	3 ft 6 in.
Rhodesia	Rhodesia Railways (R.R.)	3 ft 6 in.
Kenya	East African Railway Corporation (E.A.R.)	3 ft 3⅜ in.
Tanzania	East African Railway Corporation (E.A.R.)	3 ft 3⅜ in.

Lectures and colour shows based on this series are being given nationally. All details are available from:

Monica Gladdle
(05374) — 5179

INTRODUCTION

In this volume, I have attempted through pictures and words to show, as lucidly as possible, a remarkable aspect of a particular subject: the steam locomotive in Africa. Most engines featured are of British origin and I have discussed fairly voluminously their varied histories. But equally important are the feelings which these fascinating engines conjure up, along with the romantic aura which surrounds them. Engineers often claim there to be something basically suspect about such romanticisms; whilst an artist might claim equal awe of mechanical principles. The engineer will further state his works to be based upon sound scientific principles which are unarguable and easily enumerated, whereas the artist is merely fabricating illusions unto himself – illusions which might even be the result of an over-exerted or even slightly neurotic condition!

I hope that throughout the following pages, those made of 'sterner stuff' might come to appreciate the charm and voluptuousness of this wonderful subject. To those who already know, I can only hope that this book will invigorate their awareness and stimulate their interest.

It is not easy to put into words exactly how we feel and respond to things, nor is it easy to transmute our emotions and impressions to visual form. Given sufficient technique, the combination of words and pictures offers the artist an ultimate in communicative potential. Any shortcomings in his technique, perhaps combined with a pre-judiced attitude from the recipient, can render null the most laboriously executed works, and the artist, though possibly close to his ideal, has failed to communicate and becomes as a lost soul in a crowded city.

Poor communications are among the deep tragedies of the human condition. On all levels of activity, confusion runs wild and possibly only in the most basic formulae of scientific or practical matters do the mists thin out into any kind of absoluteness.

My journeys in Africa are reasonably well covered in the stories, but many of the people with whom I came into contact are not mentioned and I wish to include them here, because the remarkable kindness and hospitality I received from both African and European populations, did much to fortify my faith in human nature. My sincere thanks to: Monica Gladdle, Dr and Mrs Hampton, Mrs M. E. Warner, John Cross, Graham and Mary Hoare, Gordon Watson, Jim Field, Chris Butcher, Charlie Lewis, Brian Healey, David Thornhill, Horace Gamble, Panya Mohamed, Christiaan Smith, Richard Clatworthy, G. Bashford, C. H. Smith, Les Nel, R. H. Tribe, J. A. James, J. A. Cockrell, Jock Phillip, Francois Swarts, Reg Melton, Basil Bowie, Ismail Ahamed, Mohamed Swaleh, Tom Matsalia, N. G. Hedges and P. J. Odell.

Furthermore to the following organisations: South African Railways, Rhodesia Railways, East African Railways Corporation, and *World Steam* magazine, obtainable from 124 Wendover Road, Stoke Mandeville, Bucks. Lastly, my special thanks to Judy Warner for her efforts on behalf of this volume.

COLIN GARRATT

March 1974

VETRIVIER. An S.A.R. standard 15F Class 4–8–2 bursts northwards on a Bloemfontein–Kroonstad freight.

2 **OVER CROCODILE RIVER.** One of the R.R.'s Class 14ᴬ 2–6–

Beyer-Garratts ambles a goods along the West Nicholson–Bulawayo line.

3 **EXPRESS PERISHABLES.** Caught hastening through Noblesfont

of the S.A.R.'s 25c Condensing 4–8–4s with an express freight.

4 **THE CRATE.** E.A.R. 26 Class 2–8–2 No. 2611 built by Bagnall of Staffor

amed 'the crate' heads deep into the Tanzanian interior with a Tabora–Mpanda train.

5 **WILD MOMENT AT MATETSI.** The rebuilt and exorcised R.R. 15th
with tonnage for Zambia.

6-4+4-6-4 Garratt No. 404, seen here as No. 424 (see plate 38) heads towards Victoria Falls

6 **GETTING THEM MOVING (1).** An Italian-built S.A.R. 15CA Class 4–8–2 hammers its train up the bank west of Panpoort.

7 **GETTING THEM MOVING (2).** With comparable gusto an E.A.R. Class 31 Tribal 2–8–4 No. 3128 'Jopadhola' slams out of Tabora with the afternoon train to Mwanza.

8 **THE NON-CONDENSER.** Seen working a heavy De–Aar–Kimb

s is S.A.R. Class 25NC 4–8–4 No. 3401 *Anne*.

9 **GIANTS IN TANDEM.** A brace of S.A.R. 23 Cla

... ase out of Vetrivier with full tonnage for Bloemfontein.

10 **HIGH DRAMA AT WITBANK.** An unsuperheated version of the S.A.R.'s

4–8–2 erupts a glorious smokeball across the vast landscape of the Transvaal.

11 **THE GOLDFIELDS BY NIGHT.** An ex-S.A.R. Class A 4–8–2T by

...asgow takes loaded gold-ore from a shaft of the Grootvlei mine at Springs.

12 **THE BRITISH STYLE.** A North British 4–8–2T makes exciting contrast

loud flecked sky as she lifts a loaded train out of Greenside Colliery, Witbank.

13 **IMPRESSIONS AT WITBANK.** A 15AR Class 4–8–2 by Beyer Peaco⊲

5CA Class 4–8–2s reside amid the smoky intrigue of the S.A.R.'s Witbank sheds.

14 **VIADUCT ACROSS THE SEA.** Although a rather romantic notion this
The locomotive is an S.A.R. 24 Class 2–8–4.

cate something of the scenic George–Knysna branch which skirts the Indian Ocean.

15 **THE MOMBASA SPIRAL.** One of the E.A.R.'s incredible 59 Class 4–8–2+2–8–4 Garratts, No. 5922 *Mount Blackett*, leads tonnage through the hills outside Mombasa.

16 **TWO IN TANDEM.** A pair of S.A.R. 15AR Class 4–8–2s head for home with a freight from Klipplaat to Port Elizabeth.

17 **UITENHAGE EXPRESS.** No. 810 an immaculate S.A.R. 16CR Class Pacific train near Perseverance.

ngeance on the sunny skies as it hustles an eleven-coach Port Elizabeth–Uitenhage

18 **BAGNALL ON THE GOLDFIELDS.** A splendid Bagnall 4–8–2T of typ Land Exploratory Co. Springs.

appearance works a supply train over the metals of the South African

19 **THE GARRATT BOY,** who acts as third man on the engine, waters his steed in the form of an R.R. 14^A Class 2–6–2+2–6–2 Garratt seen at Balla Balla heading a We Nicholson–Bulawayo train.

VETRIVIER (2). Another S.A.R. 15F Class 4–8–2 romps northwards on a Bloemfontein–Kroonstad freight.

21   **ANIMATED SPLENDOUR.** The turbines whirr as an S.A.R. 25C Condensing

eases its merchandise back on to the main line after being looped in the Karroo.

22 **THE BALDWIN PACIFIC.** The E.P. Cement Co. of Port Elizabeth own this delig

n. gauge Baldwin Pacific seen here on night duty towards the end of its working life.

23 **PORT ELIZABETH SUBURBAN (1).** An S.A.R. Class 16CR Pacific races away from the city above the flooded waters of the Swartkops river.

PORT ELIZABETH SUBURBAN (2). Another S.A.R. Pacific, this one a 16R Class, tops the speed limit with an eleven-coach train from Uitenhage. Note the engine's ornamental smoke deflections.

25 **WATERING THE GIANT.** A Rhodesian 14^A Class 2–6–2+2–6–2 Beyer–G

... ses for refreshment at Balla Balla on its way from West Nicholson to Bulawayo.

26 **AWAITING THE COALS.** A handsome S.A.R. 12^A type 4–8–2 specially built for indus

basks in the sunshine between turns of duty at the New Douglas Colliery, Transvaal.

27 **CLASS 6 IN EXILE.** An ex Cape Government Railway 4-6-0 express passenger en

nstrates its unsuitability for industrial work at the Swartkops power station, Port Elizabeth.

28   **THE RED ENGINES OF LANDAU.** One of Landau colliery's famous re

...2s prepares for a vigorous assault on the heavy bank up to the S.A.R. main line.

29 **OBSOLESCENCE.** A brace of old British built 4–8–2T

y Dunns Engineering lie decaying in an old siding at Witbank.

30 **GARRATTS ON THE GREYTOWN LINE (2).** A GMA, leaving Harden Heig
mounts its attack on the tortuous line thirty-seven grades ahead.

31 **GARRATTS ON THE GREYTOWN LINE (3).** A detail study of the above show
how these mighty GMAs sometimes rival the once great spectacle of American stea

32 **GARRATTS ON THE GREYTOWN LINE (1).** One of the S.A.R.'s pugnacious GMA Class 4–8–2 + 2–8–4 Garratts prepares to leave New Hanover with freight for Greytown.

33 **THE STATELY 16th.** An impressive Rhodesian 16th Class 2–8–2 + 2–8–2 Garratt bu
in South Africa.

Peacock of Manchester 1929/30 finds a new lease of life at the Transvaal Navigation Colliery

34 **THE GOLDFIELDS BY NIGHT (2).** Another Scottish built 4–8–2T, this goldfields.

British of Glasgow working gold at Welkom on the southern part of South Africa's

35 **BIG GAME AT VOI.** One of the world's largest steam engines skirts the edge
Mount Londiani seen heading a 1,200-ton train for Nairobi.

o Game Reserve in the form of E.A.R. 59 Class 4–8–2+2–8–4 Garratt No. 5914

36 **ACROSS THE GREAT KARROO.** Set amid the inhospi

in of the Karroo Desert is a S.A.R. 25C Class Condensing 4–8–4.

37 **THE MIXED TRAIN.** The concept of a mixed train is well illustrated here
Klipplaat.

.. 15AR Class 4–8–2 gets into its stride with the afternoon train from Port Elizabeth to

38 EPITAPH TO A DEMON. Up in the Rhodesian hills towards the Zambian border lies the numberplate of R.R. 15th Class 4–6–4+4–6–4 Garratt No. 404, one of Africa's most ill-fated locomotives.

20th WITH BAOBAB. The ultimate in Rhodesian steam traction are the 20th Class 4–8–2 + 2–8–4 Garratts. Here one is leaving the Wankie coalfield with coal for Bulawayo and Salisbury.

40 **NAIROBI BOUND.** E.A.R. Mountain Class 59 4–8–2 + 2–8–4 Garratt No journey to Nairobi.

Suswa snakes its way round the 'S' curve west of Mombasa on the first lap of its 330-mile

41 **ERUPTION: TWO CONDENSERS DRAW UP TO THE SEMAPHO**
magnificent 25C Class Condensing 4–8–4s: among the worlds most fascin

FIRES MADE UP AND BLOWDOWN VALVES SCREAMING. The S.A.R.'s
survivors.

42 **THE WANKIE COALFIELDS.** An unsuperheated Henschel 4–8–2, belon
Her design follows that of the R.R. 19th Class and S.A.R. 19D Class.

...nkie Colliery Co. Ltd, flings up the fire as she storms across the darkened coalfields.

43 **THE ILLUSTRIOUS 4–8–2.** South Africa's staple main line power consists of
merchandise train between Kroonstad and Bloemfontein.

Class 4–8–2s, the most numerous African type. Here one is seen wheeling a southbound

44 **MONOLITHS.** A standard North British 4–8–2T delivers coal t

r station from the adjacent New Largo Colliery in South Africa's Transvaal.

45 **RAW ACTION.** With turbine fan whining and blowdown fully on, one of the S.A
express.

lible 25C Class Condensing 4–8–4s muses its way over the Karroo with a northbound

46 **BOX FREIGHT FROM KILIMANJARO.** An E.A.R. 60 Class *Governor* 4–8–2+2–
named *Sir James Hayes-Sadler*.

...att heads for Voi with an overnight freight from Moshi. This engine was formerly

47　**SWAN-SONG OF THE CLASS 8.** A surviving remnant of the Cape Govern
SWCM Collieries, Transvaal.

is the British built ex-S.A.R. Class 8 4–8–0 seen here on one of its final duties for the

48 **SOUTHWARDS FROM SHINYANGA.** No. 3013 *Makua*, an E.A.R. 30 Class Trit 2–8–4, leaves for Tabora with a goods from Mwanza on the shore of Lake Victoria Tanzania.

S.A.R. 15CA Class 4–8–2 Plates Nos. 6, 13

Of the comparatively few American-built locomotives to be found on South Africa's railways, perhaps the most significant are these 15CA/15CB 4–8–2s, along with their close relations the passenger-hauling 16D/16DA pacifics. Although remarkably modern in looks, these 4–8–2s date back to 1925, some 50 years ago, to a time when, after considerable research, it was decided to try out some large American-type engines on the South African railways. Thus, in 1925, two 15C Class 4–8–2s were delivered to Cape Town from Baldwins Locomotive Works: they proved to be excellent performers and the Company received an order for a further ten a few months later. Hefty engines for their day, the 15Cs promptly acquired the nickname of 'Big Bills'. In 1926 a slightly improved version came from the works of A.L.C.O. (American Locomotive Company) and this led to the differentiation of 15C*A* for the A.L.C.O. engines and 15C*B* for the Baldwin ones, although ostensibly the two types are identical. This improvement was necessary for, despite the remarkable prowess with which the 15Cs went about their duties, some trouble was encountered with frame fractures around their firebox area and this problem was rectified in the A.L:C.O. engines. After the initial twelve engines from Baldwins all subsequent building, including later engines from that Company, was to the 15CA pattern. Altogether 96 were built, 39 in America, 10 by Breda of Italy and the remaining 47 from North British of Glasgow. By 1930, five years after their inception, all 96 had been put into traffic and so was formed one of the S.A.R.'s principal classes, a class which was regarded as being a natural successor to the 15A 4–8–2s introduced in 1914 (see page 145).

Over the years modifications have been made to the driving wheel and cylinder diameters which have been increased by 3 in. and 1 in. respectively. This was done under Watson's régime as C.M.E. of the S.A.R. in the early 1930s, for he believed bigger wheel diameters meant greater mileages between shoppings. These modifications, combined with a slight increase in boiler pressure, meant that the tractive effort remained virtually unaffected. Apparently this was also to enhance the class's ability to a level commensurate with the 15F 4–8–2s (see page 115) but one fundamental difference remained in that most 15Fs are mechanically stoked whereas none of the American-designed engines are, accordingly they have never been capable of such sustained power outputs.

The first engines went into service between Cape Town and Kimberley, later spreading to Bloemfontein and Johannesburg for main line mixed traffic operation. Today however, most are found at Capital Park depot, Pretoria, from which they operate up to Pietersburg and Witbank, the latter route affording them complete monopoly of traffic to which end Witbank depot is also well endowed with their abilities.

My first acquaintance with the 15CAs was at Capital Park depot, Pretoria, one of the Republic's largest steam depots. Here I became accustomed to their pleasantly rounded features which made a striking contrast with the angular lines of the more modern 15Fs also in abundance. Most of the active 15CAs were working out to Witbank, consequently to facilitate seeing them in action I ventured eastwards over the Transvaal in that direction. This single line carries no mean traffic density, hence the provision of innumerable crossing loops, one of these being situated at Panpoort, an isolated hamlet lying about halfway between the two cities. I suppose Panpoort would rate as one of those places which frequently gets one into trouble when touring with other people, for so captivating was its atmosphere and so satisfying did I find the 15CAs, which pounded their way up and down all day long, that I rather forgot my itinerary and became lost in the strange charm of this lonely place. In fact some days had passed before I could muster up an urge to leave and even then it was with a heavy heart, so alluring was its almost magical individuality.

This line, like so many in South Africa, undulates like a sheet of corrugated iron – and how the 15CAs pound over it! Their harsh staccato exhausts being audible miles across country, for they are said to have the loudest exhausts of all S.A.R. classes – a saying well borne out by my observations. Their behaviour almost defies description for they charge furiously up the banks with a sharp, spitting beat not unlike the sound of a drumstick striking a tightly stretched snare drum, whereupon gaining the summit, they fall completely silent and coast down the other side. Such vigorous operation is well testified by the many slip lacerations and indentations on the rails. An interesting range of traffic traverses this line, especially coal from the vast Witbank coalfields, but also chrome ore for exportation from Lourenco Marques. Explosive trains can be seen coming from the Modderfontein factory near Pretoria, whilst in the other direction oil trains come up from Lourenco Marques in addition to vegetable, fruit and timber trains from the eastern Low Veld. Furthermore, there is quite an extensive pig traffic from Pienarspoort where the Republic's largest pig farm is situated. Passenger trains also appear; the principal ones being the Pretoria to Lourenco Marques expresses which are 15CA operated as far as Witbank, thenceforwards electric traction assumes control.

My only chance of comfort amid the wild and sparsely populated area of Panpoort was in an hotel some miles away, from which, throughout the forthcoming nights, I was destined to hear the 15CAs in action. Having arrived at the hotel in good time for the evening meal I was ready by first light the following day to seek out the subject of my attentions. Having reached the railway I made my way down the track towards the lonely crossing operator's cabin, for I had been in South Africa but three days and was naturally anxious to meet some inhabitants, as well as glean some information on the railway. Although having been noted by the cabin's solitary occupant long before I actually reached the door, I was nevertheless greeted by more than a glint of surprise, if not actually suspicion. Unashamedly I announced my business, presenting my camera as additional credibility. I quickly realised that my new acquaintance was too polite deliberately to express any surprise at my intentions but nonetheless he was somewhat taken aback, as his slightly distrustful countenance and reserved manner indicated. It is moments such as these which forceably remind one that specialised researches are often difficult to understand, especially to people living in different cultures from one's own. Happily, my behaviour and presence were soon taken at their face value and my new friend announced himself as Louis Van Wyk. He proved to be a man of lively disposition, his pensive air being well suited to the quiet, rugged country in which Panpoort is set. So began some enchanting days with the 15CAs, during which time no other class of engine appeared on this busy line. Quite apart from the engines, one of the line's most palatable qualities was its 100 per cent steam operation, though infinitely less exciting is its scheduled transfer over to electric traction by 1975; the poles and wires already having been erected over certain stretches.

Without abashment I would claim that Louis soon became glad of my company, so lonely was his cabin, and eventually I became pounded by many questions about Britain and its railways, the slant of his enquiries indicating one anxious to elucidate many points of hearsay. During one conversation my companion indicated a strange V opening cut into the heavy wire fence which isolates the S.A.R. from the surrounding countryside. This opening was immediately opposite

Louis' cabin and he explained that the V symbolised victory and was specially cut for Britain's Royal family when they visited South Africa in 1946, immediately after World War II. Apparently they had spent a night on board their train in Panpoort loop and the opening was made to facilitate a morning walk prior to the train's departure and no one had ever joined up the fencing since.

The all-steam atmosphere of Panpoort conjured up images of Britain's main lines prior to their modernisation and our many discussions graduated to a level similar to those recorded by the railway photographer Eric Treacy. I thought in particular of the stories in his classic work 'Steam Up' when, in his own inimitable way, he recounted some of his adventures and acquaintances whilst photographing from the linesides of northern England. My experiences, in essence, seemed the same, for between trains my discussions with Louis ranged over many topics from locomotives, ethics, politics – especially the apartheid question – through to nature. The last gave emphasis to the many birds which inhabited the crossing area, most being indigenous to Africa and thus totally new to me. Throughout my stay the conversations and photography were interspersed with Louis' special Panpoort brew which he unstintingly produced at the most appropriate moments.

A sombre note cut into this idyllic situation: my friend's continued warnings of cobras and puff adders. Never will I forget his tale of the night when a huge cobra entered the cabin unseen and entangled itself amongst the signal lever frame. How long it had been there is unknown for it was not until Louis turned to accept an approaching train that he saw the hideous thing, simultaneously realising, to his horror, that quite apart from being unable to pull off the signal it was also risky to attempt leaving the cabin for fear the vicious reptile should lash out at him. Eventually it was beaten to death but not until the train had been held for some minutes and the fireman was on his way down the line to ascertain the problem. As I set out to make plate 6 Louis called after me, 'That bank up there's full of them,' but fortunately none were encountered! The engine is 2807, one of the Italian-built Bredas of 1929 and I was interested to note that she was still attached to an Italian-built tender.

The 15CAs were also seen to good advantage in the smoky atmosphere at Witbank engine sheds where quite a number are based (plate 13). This picture is in marked contrast to the sunny lineside work in the hope that it evokes some other facets of the steam age's magical appeal. Possibly one might almost smell the oil, soot and vapour set against the mystical potion of sunlight streaming through the blackened windows.

	15CB	
No. Series	Builder	Date
2060–2071	Baldwin	1925

	15CA	
No. Series	Builder	Date
2039–2059	A.L.C.O.	1926
2072–2073	A.L.C.O.	1926
2074–2077	Baldwin	1929
2801–2810	Breda	1929
2811–2839	North British	1928/29
2840–2857	North British	1930

Leading Dimensions

Cylinders	24 in. × 28 in.
Boiler pressure	210 lb per sq. in.
Driving wheel diameter	5 ft 0 in.
Grate area	48 sq. ft
Tractive effort at 85% b.p.	47,980 lb
Total length	approx. 73 ft 2 in.
Total weight f.w.o.	approx. 173 tons

SOUTH AFRICAN COLLIERIES: 12A Type Unsuperheated 4–8–2   Plates Nos. 10, 26, 28

The colliery railways of South Africa often employ ex-main line engines of considerable power, so contrasting with many countries where smaller, specially built locomotives suffice. However the difficult terrain of Africa, combined with long hauls from colliery to main line, necessitates the employment of large engines and adequately justifies the phenomenon. This power can sometimes aspire to the heights of 2–8–2 + 2–8–2 Garratts as testified by plate 33, but perhaps more typical are these 12A 4–8–2s which are one of the Republic's more standardised colliery engines and as such provide an aura of cohesion against the plethora of multi-hued relics which inhabit the complex of mines around Witbank and other major coal producing areas in South Africa.

The Witbank collieries have an unusual air about them, for they are set in rich farmland on the flat table-like expanse which typifies this area of the Transvaal. Maize crops predominate, alternated by grass-veld, both under the guardianship of a vast sky in which may be seen smoke trails from distant engines as they undertake their workaday chores on various colliery networks. Indeed the density of collieries around Witbank indicates that this is the Republic's richest coal-producing area, the seams hereabouts being immensely thick. If in some collieries the locomotive variety is rather standardised, then full compensation is made by the liveries, which range from black to chocolate via red, green, blue and other hues less easily enumerated.

The heavily industrialised coal and iron town of Witbank is said to constitute South Africa's most polluted region yet the town centre itself sports a sparkling air of modernity. A few miles out of town are found the collieries of Landau and Wolverkrans, the former possessing maroon engines, whilst the latter's are gaily decked in Caledonian Blue. Both collieries operate 12A classes as evidenced by plates 10, 28 although Landau is further noted for its ex-Rhodesian Railways 16th Class Garratt, whilst the Witbank Colliery Company – who operate Wolverkrans – further reward the observer with some North British-built 4–8–2Ts, usually in resplendent condition.

Possibly this system is one of the most famous in the entire Republic as the lines from Landau and Wolverkrans join up for a mile or two before diverging away to their respective exchange sidings with the S.A.R. Thus one can enjoy – or perhaps more correctly – has the potential of enjoying, for the R.R. 16th Class Garratt was in shops at the time of my visit, 12As, 4–8–2Ts, and Garratts featuring maroon and blue liveries along with different styles of lettering, all over one stretch of railway. The plates echo this for No. 28 depicts one of Landau's 12As emerging from the woods and approaching the junction with the Wolverkrans line, while plate 10 shows Witbank Colliery Co.'s No. 4, of the same class, heading across the stretch of common track. This latter picture illustrates the Transvaal's thrilling spaciousness and typifies the terrain amid which these industrial lines are set. The vastness is echoed by the African sky whilst the unconventional placing of the subject is tempered by the inky smoke-ball which looms ominously above the golden vegetation, so balancing the locomotive in a kind of geometrical see-saw.

One may gain the impression that the 12As are principally a colliery locomotive, but actually the first ones appeared on the S.A.R.

as early as 1919 being Hendrie's larger version of his earlier 12 Class. Even in those days they worked coal around Witbank especially to Germiston, being able to cope with 1,400-ton trains. Between 1919/1929 the S.A.R. put 67 12As into traffic: principally they came from North British in Glasgow, but a few also emanated from Henschel of Germany. From 1943 onwards massive round top boilers were fitted, so creating the 12AR variants, but only about 45 engines have been so modified, the rest remaining unaltered. Modifications aside, it is no small testimony to the superlative qualities enacted by the 12As that some 35 years after their inception the type should still be built for collieries, albeit in an unsuperheated form as specified by the industrial establishments. These colliery engines, which were built well into the 1950s, were also from North British and they exist today alongside their main line counterparts of 50 years ago.

I must recount the wonderful tale of the Witbank Colliery Company No. 4. During World War II this company's Scottish engineer ordered their first 12A from North British of Glasgow suggesting that she be painted in Caledonian Blue. This was done and the engine was duly shipped out but was unfortunately sunk by a German U-Boat during transit. It was not until 1947 that a replacement engine arrived and this engine, also painted in Caledonian Blue, was delivered in twenty huge wooden packing cases which were unceremoniously placed in the shed yard at Witbank for the attention of the colliery engineer! This posed a mammoth construction job, as no overhead crane was available and the subsequent endeavours to construct No. 4 are still discussed at Witbank to this day.

Three Europeans, one an apprentice, and eight African workers were duly assigned to execute the task: the apprentice was the Company's present-day engineer Mr Hunter. After unpacking the crates, No. 4's anatomy soon became evident and some initial collation was undertaken before the business of construction began. Only manual power and jacks were available: first the frames were jacked up with sleepers and the wheels rolled underneath. The boiler was likewise jacked up with sleepers then miraculously jacked across girders until it hovered precariously over the frames: further jacking enabled the girders to be removed and the boiler lowered into its seating. Setting the boiler into place took three continuous days of blood, sweat and toil – not to mention tears! Twenty-three days after unpacking the crates a resplendent No. 4 stood in steam at Witbank, her safety valves singing and the engine raring to go.

Mr Hunter has, in his home, a wonderful framed colour photograph depicting the newly completed engine with the eleven-man team proudly standing alongside: additionally his family photo album has two pages of pictures devoted to the various stages commencing with the twenty assorted boxes and ending with a fine action picture of No. 4 on the road. Railwaymen often become endeared towards certain locomotives for all manner of reasons but few can be more poignant than Mr Hunter's regard for No. 4 as, to this day, almost thirty years later, both man and machine are still together at the Witbank depot.

During the early 1950s Witbank Colliery Company took delivery of another 12A from North British but this one was assembled in a rather more dignified manner by Dunns Engineering Ltd, Witbank. Even using proper overhead cranes and a much larger team of men the operation still took seven days! The new engine became No. 5 and, of course, worked as sister engine to No. 4, although Mr Hunter insists most vehemently, and presumably without bias, that No. 4 has always been the superior engine and is, at best, capable of taking almost half as much again as No. 5! I personally did not see No. 5 as she was in Dunns for overhaul at the time of my visit.

On the graded run from Wolverkrans these 4–8–2s are expected to haul about 900-ton trains, although when the Company tried out an ex-R.R. 16th Class Garratt, loaned to them pending sale from Dunns, they found this giant could walk away with 1,500 tons and more. However a likelihood of extra maintenance problems decided Witbank Colliery to remain with their faithful 12As although, as previously mentioned, the neighbouring Landau Colliery does operate a Garratt as well.

The Witbank engines handle over 24,000 tons of coal per week from Wolverkrans. A heavy tonnage also emanates from Landau, whose coal after a special double washing process to glean the finest possible quality, is exported to Japan via Lourenco Marques.

Leading Dimensions

Cylinders	24 in × 26 in.
Boiler pressure	190 lb per sq. in.
Driving wheel diameter	4 ft 3 in.
Grate area	41 sq. ft
Tractive effort 85% b.p.	47,420 lb
Total length	approx. 70 ft
Total weight f.w.o.	approx. 165 tons

Transvaal Colliery

SOUTH AFRICAN INDUSTRIAL: North British 4–8–2T
Plates Nos. 12, 44

Over the last century Britain has been such a prolific exporter of steam engines that the 'British look' can still be seen in many parts of the world. I spare the reader any attempt to define the 'British look' and suffice to say that these 4–8–2Ts appear more British than did a good many indigenous designs. Purely an industrial machine, these splendid engines abound throughout South Africa's collieries, especially around Witbank, but also on the Natal coalfield. As handsome an engine as one could wish for, they furthermore sport a fine range of liveries – green, chocolate, red or blue. Produced by the North British Locomotive Co. of Glasgow, the class is now an industrial standard and so typical are they, that the Republic's 5 Rand note depicts a hybridised version of one in the form of a 4–10–2T set amid a gold mine environment, so evoking some of the country's industrial atmosphere.

These 4–8–2Ts are a sophisticated version of the nineteenth-century Dubs 'H' Class of the Natal Government Railway and although the Hs were once 4–10–2s, their eventual demotion from main line service produced a modification to 4–8–2T, whilst further demotions over more recent years have taken many into industrial use. The North British also built many Hs; in fact they have been responsible for a high

97

percentage of South African engines in general. This Company, which arose from the merger of Neilson Co., Dubs and Sharp Roberts in 1903, built over 26,000 steam locomotives – more than any other European maker – and sent them to all corners of the world, especially Europe, India, British Colonies, South America, China and Japan, in addition to many African countries.

These 4–8–2Ts were built with a moderate axle load to suit rails weighing 60 lb per yard which in itself is fairly light, although a gap was allowed in the framing for the addition of an extra driving axle for operation over 45 lb per yard track. Apart from the basic 4–8–2T some almost identical 4–8–4Ts were also built as prospective purchasers were invited by North British to specify the exact nature of their requirements along with details of track strength, curves and gradient profiles. The 4–8–4T variant, of which over a dozen were built, differ visibly in that their side tanks were reduced in length, extra water being carried towards the rear of the engine. These extra trailing wheels created less stress on the trailing axle and made for much smoother running. Built between 1937 and 1955, these 4–8–2Ts can easily lift trains weighing over 400 tons away from a stand on a 1 in 50 gradient.

I think *Monoliths* (plate 44) indicates the essence of this class, for I have tried to show the engine as a vibrant industrial machine and to combine the industrial environment's intensity almost to a point of romanticism. Further potency is provided by the engine's acrid smoke mixing with the vapours rising from the cooling towers juxtaposed against the complementary hue of a tranquil sky. I regard chocolate as one of the most distinctive and satisfying liveries for a locomotive; does it not create a gleeful feeling? New Largo Colliery has two 4–8–2Ts, Nos. 1 and 2, both built in 1951, whilst No. 3 is a 4–8–4T and was built in 1950. As is often the case however, the engines vary within themselves every bit as much as by mechanical variations, and No. 1 has always been by far the best engine, it being claimed that she can take one third more train weight than No. 2; a prowess which also serves to eclipse engine No. 3.

Now contrast these New Largo engines with their blushing sister at Greenside Colliery, plate 12, for she contrasts not just in livery, but also environment, being set against the delicate beauty of lineside grasses and a mottled sky. The forlorn figure sitting on the engine is not unlike a character from a Dickens novel. He introduces a note of joylessness into an otherwise radiant scene. He is the 'sandboy', an

African labourer whose job is to sit on the engine's buffer beam with a barrel of sand and spray the rails in front of the engine to minimise slipping when pulling heavy loads, and is in effect an auxiliary to the locomotive's main sanding gear.

It so happened that these 4–8–2Ts provided South Africa's railways with some of their most hybridised freaks. Certainly the basic design built by North British is as sane and rational looking as any engine could be, but many collieries decided to convert them to tender engines, often with bizarre results, whilst the theory behind such conversions was sane enough, the practicable angle could be somewhat open to question. For instance, the Springbok Colliery possesses one converted to a 4–8–0, which runs minus its side-tanks and coupled to the most unlikely looking four-wheeled tender – an incredible piece of ironmongery manufactured at Landau, unashamedly lettered with gay abandon 'SPRINGBOK COLLIERY NO. 1'. The unlikely looks of this creation are well supported by practice; as the tender is affixed by a normal buffer joint welded onto a thin buffer beam, the unhappy locomotive cannot pull anything. Any attempt would promptly rip the whole concoction apart because the buffer beam is not fixed to the framing! This tender does not carry coal, the engine's original bunker being retained for this purpose. Were this the sum total of the aberration one might consider certain adjectives formerly used in describing it as being over-emphatic, but I hasten to add, it was not, for when the side-tanks were removed, it was found that insufficient adhesion rendered the abased locomotive next to useless, thus it was decided to build false splashers on the running plates and fill them, on either side, with $3\frac{1}{2}$ tons of waste steel mixed with $1\frac{1}{2}$ tons of concrete, so reconstituting the adhesion loss. Whatever was the reason for such antics? Simply that water leaking from the side tanks of the original 4–8–2Ts promoted heavy slipping by wetting both the wheels and rails, furthermore the engines never seemed to have quite the adhesion necessary for heavy work – especially when water levels were low. Of course, this latter problem might have been successfully overcome by adding weights to the tanks, but this would have heightened the centre of gravity to a potentially dangerous level, whilst compensation sought by adjusting the springing would have incurred spring breakages owing to the exceptionally rough track encountered on industrial lines. When seen in such a form, the character of the original 4–8–2T is completely absent, but in every conversion one can always recognise the individualistic cylinder shaping and so identify the engine's origin. Sometimes the cab and bunker outlines are also obvious although in many cases the bunkers have been completely removed.

Paradoxically, these hybridised locomotives are almost as common as the original 4–8–2Ts and it is interesting to record the different reasons for conversion, because some mines have blamed surging water in the engines' side-tanks for inducing excess stress on axle boxes and coupling rod joints, whilst other reasons given were a simple desire to increase coal and water capacities: which in some cases were certainly too low if the engines were needed to run long distances with heavy trains. An example of this latter point is illustrated by Tweefontein Collier's No. 3 N.B.L. 4–8–2T No. 26244 of 1948. Below is a comparison of holding capacity before and after conversion.

As 4–8–2T
Coal	4 tons
Water	1,720 gallons

As 4–8–0 with ex Main Line XF type tender
Coal	10 tons
Water	3,000 gallons

Leading Dimensions Standard 4–8–2T
Cylinder	20 in. × 24 in.
Boiler pressure	180 lb per sq. in.
Driving wheel diameter	3 ft 9½ in.
Grate area	25 sq. ft
Tractive effort 85% b.p.	32,280 lb
Total length	40 ft
Total weight f.w.o.	77 tons (52 tons on coupled wheels)

Ex S.A.R. Class 8 4–8–0   Plate No. 47

It was late morning as I wandered across the grassy veld towards the exchange sidings at Saaiwater. The sun beamed intermittently from a cloud-flecked sky, lighting up both the yellow vegetation and distant colliery tips which looked almost purple through the haze of an African winter's day. I was in no hurry, there was time enough to reach the sidings before the gaunt black-clad Class 7 engine was due to arrive with a trainload of freshly-lifted coals from the nearby

Witbank Consolidated Colliery. The going was rough, for although the grass was little more than a foot high the ground beneath was rocky and uneven; I assumed it to have been subjected to some past industrial disturbance. After a while I noticed, some 250 yards away, a road which ran parallel to my chosen direction and I decided to forsake the veld and turned towards the band of orange dust which was leading to Saaiwater. Apart from easier walking, the security of a road meant freedom from snakes for even at that time of year they were not uncommon, especially when the sun was high.

Upon gaining the road, I proceeded at twice the pace, musing contentedly as I did so on the air's remarkable clarity, for despite this being designated as an industrial region one could, to all intents and purposes, be lost amid the grassy plains of centuries past for all the intrusion the industrial complex made upon the general scene.

My musings were interrupted by the high speed approach of two huge coal lorries raising the most hideous pall of dust in their wake and threatening me with suffocation. I was forced to leave the road at right angles and return to the veld in an effort to avoid the impact. I had scarcely gone 25 yards when the first lorry swirled by and although I was out of range of the pebbles which flew from its wheels with a gun-like velocity, I was smothered by the enormous dust cloud. The second lorry repeated the performance, which a mischievous wind blew in my direction.

With the tornado now a mere speck in the distance I returned to the road remonstrating with myself for the lack of foresight which allowed such a thing to happen as the dust had badly stung my eyes, and covered my clothes. I could hardly have induced a worse effect had I physically rolled in the fluffy dust heaps which collected along the road's verges. I proceeded, with the thought that if my Class 7 threw up half as much effect as those lorries a good picture would surely result!

Before Saaiwater came into sight, a railway line suddenly curved in from my right hand side and ran along adjacent to the road, presumably heading for the same destination, and I fell to wondering what line it could be. Was it a shale tip extension from Witbank Consolidated Colliery? If so, there was no sign of it in the direction from which the line had come. Whatever it was, I reflected, it was well used, as the gleaming rails clearly evidenced. Notwithstanding the many possibilities, I rather convinced myself that it was some part of the Consolidated's network and was thus operated by the Class 7

101

engines which were the subject of my preoccupations and in this somewhat casual vein I continued my journey. But a surprise awaited me, for soon afterwards the rhythmical throb of an approaching steam train was to be heard. Turning expectantly I saw a grey cloud of exhaust puttering skywards and although the engine was, as yet, invisible, the heavy booming of its exhaust did more than hold my attention. Soon the chunky outline of a friendly, robust-looking engine came into sight attractively decked in silver, green and red; here was no repetition of a Class 7 but a completely new type quite unknown to me. Bursting with action and colour and as handsome an engine as I had yet encountered, the stranger rolled past, followed by her long line of coal-laden waggons. Animated by excitement, I broke into a run, not with any intention to match the train, but simply to reach Saaiwater exchange before the engine departed, for I realised from this brief encounter that I had seen my first Class 8 4–8–0.

This was the sparkling engine of plate 47, a picture made later that day. Thenceforth my attentions remained with the Class 8 for considerable filming had already been undertaken with the related Class 7s. Half an hour after first seeing the engine I was on board at Saaiwater as she wheezily collated empties for her return journey. I proffered a divisional photographic permit to the driver who promptly regarded this sufficient authority for me to remain on board, and so it was that I journeyed back with the Class 8, to an unknown destination; for after diverging away from the road previously described, we set off across a flat grassy plain, already well singed and scorched by our engine's past endeavours. Soon we struck a heavy bank; the down-grade of this must have helped the engine attain the bustling momentum with which it had passed me earlier. Slowed now to a walking pace, the laboured exhaust beats were quickened only by a trace of slipping as we bit into the bank, the train's resistance noticeably increasing with every few yards of progress. Save for these odd bouts of slipping the Class 8 was to prove master of the occasion, but not without speed being reduced to a crawl and an agonising gap occurring between each tortured exhaust beat. I was chatting to the driver when he casually indicated towards the lineside fence and, following his inclination, I saw to my horror an enormous headless snake entwined about the meshing. My expression caused him to laugh. 'Not poisonous,' he interjected, 'I don't know why they kill them!' My earlier fears of snakes had now been more than substantiated, but they were soon forgotten as the Class 8 quickened pace, her battle won, and she now jubilantly rolled downgrade towards the housings of the South Witbank Consolidated Mine where she belonged.

We drew to a shuddering stop and I dismounted into the industrial tapestry which formed the colliery yard. There was half an hour to wait before the Class 8 took the last train of the day down to Saaiwater exchange and as it had already been agreed that I should again accompany the crew I set about some intermediate explorations of my new environment. There was activity everywhere; apparently the colliery operated throughout 24 hours, although its Class 8 was usually dormant during the night. After looking around I sat myself down upon a heap of coal and contentedly awaited the green engine to attach itself to a string of loaded waggons which stood on a nearby embankment. After about an hour she appeared and I made my way to the place where they were coupling up.

I scrambled up the embankment to rail level, emerging at a point just in front of the buffer beam and walked alongside the engine intending to climb into the cab. Suddenly, with the force of a violent explosion the blowdown valve was turned fully on just as I drew level with it. I do not know whether my greatest concern was the heat of the water and steam which enveloped me or the incredible force with which it emanated. Clutched in the arms of a swirling white monster, I was lifted from my feet and flung back down the bank, choked by steam and stung by blinding grit deflected upwards off the soily bank. I felt I was falling down a mountainside in an avalanche, with the roar of crashing rocks all about me. The bank seemed like an endless chasm, through which I was being blasted to eternity. At the bottom of the bank the steam began to thin out, and my relief at seeing the blue sky appear through the evaporating wisps might be akin to that of one rescued after being trapped underground for hours. Covered in sludge, coal dust and soil, and completely soaked, I proceeded with brazen agony back up the bank. All was quiet now, for the engine, having done its worst, was simmering demurely in the sunshine, looking to all intents and purposes incapable of producing such a paroxysm.

'Wherever have you been?' called the driver as he caught sight of my bedraggled form. 'I was caught by the blowdown,' was my reply – and I confess that it contained more than a hint of vindictiveness! He leapt from the cab and rushed to enquire if I was hurt. Physically I had few ills to report, save for the mess I was in along with that of my camera, which looked as though it had been dipped into a vat of coal sludge: to think that I had ever cursed the innocent meanderings of

103

two coal lorries! The driver, avidly blaming himself, hastened me to the warmth of the engine, augmenting my relief as he did so by telling of a colleague who was once blinded by a blowdown valve.

This device is a prominent feature of many African locomotives, it being designed to eject chemical impurities from their boilers. African water contains many unsuitable constituents which would quickly erode the tubes, boiler and fireboxes if ignored. These impurities tend to concentrate around the bottom of the boiler and so are periodically blasted out into the atmosphere at full boiler pressure by means of a blowdown valve. This ejection takes place at right angles from the engine and crews have to exercise great care before blowing down – for the reasons I have illustrated! Some main line depots possess special blowdown 'ducts', formed of brick, such as the one at De Aar. Plates 36, 45, whilst demonstrating the aesthetic aspects of blowdown also give a good idea of its thrust.

With my clothes steaming almost as well as the Class 8 we set off for Saaiwater. Conversation was limited by the engine rattling: she was not in good order, the play in her axle boxes being such that she jigged around on her wheels in a rather alarming way. 'Don't think she will last much longer,' shouted the driver, 'Three months at most!'

By the time we began the heavy climb back with empties the sun was reduced to a quickly disappearing vermilion ball throwing the veld into bluish gold shadow. The sharpness of an African winter's night was beginning to be apparent, especially as the only movements I could make, perched atop the tender, were a series of deft contortions to avoid being struck by branches which overhung the railway. Weird sounds emanated from our engine whenever she was under strain and these alarmed a flock of guinea fowl feeding in the lineside stubble. With yelping cries they rose 'en masse' in silhouette against a muted sunset, their shapes rivalled by the blobs of exhaust exuding unashamedly from the Class 8.

Darkness had fallen by the time I left the engine, which by now was already on the ashpits having her fire dropped. As I walked away up the gloomy hillside I could hear the pricker grinding amongst the firebars, and pausing to look back I saw her bathed in a vivid orange inferno as the blazing cinders rained out of her. Soon she whistled up to proceed into the shed, the ever-diminishing steam pressure now rendering her whistle flat, toneless and rather sad. Thus closed my experience with the Class 8, perhaps the only one I might ever see, because after some 70 years' service, their place belongs in history and my chubby, handsomely-decked friend was already one of the last in service. I turned once more to gaze over the now blackened countryside and I could still discern the colliery lights and hear the rattling of coals as they dropped from the washery conveyor belt into the empty waggons waiting beneath. These waggons would also wait for the Class 8 which, fey as she was, would whisk them away to Saaiwater the following morning.

The Class's origin lies in a set of transatlantic 2–8–0s acquired by the Cape Government Railway (C.G.R.) in 1901 from Schenectady and Alco. This type was perpetuated, but as a 4–8–0, so giving birth to the 8 Class, all of which came from British builders despite retaining rather Americanised looks along with such American characteristics as bar frames and high running plate. Although initially put into traffic under Beatty, C.M.E. of the C.G.R., they were almost simultaneously constructed for the Imperial Military Railway (I.M.R.). The engines were quickly absorbed into the Central South African Railway (C.S.A.R.) which covered the railways in the Orange Free State and Transvaal. Further examples were built for this administration under its C.M.E., Hyde. Regarded as a mixed traffic class, the 8s were for many years important main line power over much of South Africa.

Basically some 175 were built, all between 1902/4, coming from Neilson and North British; Neilson having become part of North British during the interim period. None survive on the main lines today, the remnants all existing in industry.

Class 8 4–8–0 Batches

8	C.G.R.	23 built	1902/3	
8A	I.M.R.	40 ,,	1902	
8B	C.S.A.R.	30 ,,	1903	
8C	C.S.A.R.	30 ,,	1903	
8D	C.G.R.	38 ,,	1903	
8E	C.G.R.	4 ,,	1903	(originally larger grates but later rebuilt to conformity)
8F	C.G.R.	10 ,,	1904	

Despite innumerable variations such as the addition of superheaters, piston valves and long travel piston valves, the Class's basic dimensions may be assumed as follows:

105

Cylinders	18½ in. × 24 in.
Boiler pressure	180 lb per sq. in.
Driving wheel diameter	4 ft 0 in.
Grate area	21 sq. ft
Tractive effort 85% b.p.	26,180 lb
Total length	54 ft approx.
Total weight f.w.o.	103 tons

Ex S.A.R. Dubs 'A' 4–8–2T   **Plate No. 11**
                                                          Front endpaper
Ex S.A.R. Dubs 'B' (Class G) 4–8–2T   **Plate No. 29**

For almost half a century the Natal Government Railway was operated by tank engines, the Class A 4–8–2Ts being possibly their most ubiquitous and best loved design. Certainly it is no exaggeration to say that this Class, along with their close relations the B and the H Classes, have been one of South Africa's classic locomotive types and although now extinct on main line service, many still survive at various industrial establishments where they are enjoying a new lease of life – despite the fact that 86 years have passed since the first examples were put into traffic on the N.G.R.! Made up of 100 engines, the entire A Class was delivered by Dubs & Co., Glasgow, between 1888 and 1900. At their inception the As were put into traffic by W. Milne, but satisfaction with the design led to their perpetuation under G. W. Reid who took over as Locomotive Superintendent in 1896. However, after Hendrie's accession in 1903 some detail alterations were made giving them Belpair fireboxes with wider grates along with a better cab design and these were simply known as 'improved As'. Actually the Class totalled 102 engines by virtue of a couple which were built at Durban Workshops during World War I. This was a period when more locomotives were needed, but supplies from abroad were difficult to obtain and some mitigation of the adversity was achieved by the discovery of sufficient spares to make up a couple of complete engines. Both were placed in service during 1915.

Possibly the best place to see the As in traffic is on the metals of the Grootvlei Proprietary Mines, an important gold-producing concern at Springs, it being over this system that the plates were made. Three reside here and are kept in lovely condition; two of them came direct from the S.A.R. in the mid 1930s whilst the third emanated from the African and European Investment Co. in 1941. Usually only one engine is in traffic at a time and her principal duty is hauling gold ore from the mine to the reduction plant, although intermittently she breaks off these duties to operate workmen's passenger trains over various parts of the system, hauling as she does so a motley array of vintage stock.

The Company is rather proud of these As and in 1970 published the following statistics regarding them: 'Some 4,000 tons of gold ore were carried daily and since being commissioned the engines have, between them, moved some $40\frac{1}{4}$ million tons of ore, having run over one million miles during the process.' Accurate or not, such figures are interesting assessments and demonstrate the tremendous utility of old main line locomotives sold to industry.

The endpaper features a Grootvlei A Class juxtaposed with the gold workings, the duplication of smoking chimneys adding both cohesion and credibility to the scene. Notice the engine's first dome; this was typical N.G.R. practice and is known as the 'sugar pot' but is of course a sand container. Some are running today with this innovation removed, like the A at East Daggafontein Gold Mine, which now has a steam-driven electricity generator attached to the sand dome bracket. A number of locomotive engineers have said that a second dome spoils an engine's appearance but, for me, the 'sugar pots' must remain – note it again on the ex N.G.R. H tank, rear endpaper! I also think the As are more than a little enhanced visually by the placing of their clack valves in the cab from which an internal delivery pipe passes through the boiler. Practically, these internal feed pipes are not a good thing as they become badly scaled over, although aesthetically they are greatly to be preferred to the ungainly outside feed pipes of most S.A.R. engines. Finally, plate 11 depicts one on night duty, for such is the demand for gold that this engine was working continually throughout 24 hours and only returned to shed for fire raking and bunkering up. See how her smokebox is stained with gold ore after passing beneath the loading shaft. Such activity is supported by the fact that some 70% of the Free World's annual supply of newly mined gold comes from South Africa.

Whilst at Springs I saw the As hauling gold throughout the night. African labourers rode the hopper waggon ends with blazing braziers made from huge punched barrels, so cold were the winter evenings. It was a thrilling sight to watch the veteran engine clanking its gold laden waggons, for despite all the romantic connotations commonly associated with this metal, it still commences its existence with nineteenth century steam engines. I observed many night hauls as she rolled along the rickety track from the loading shaft, bouncing cinders in all directions and followed by her ghostly string of waggons intermittently illuminated with dancing fire from the braziers. One could just discern the animated expressions and umbery tones of the labourers' faces before the whole fabulous procession disappeared away through the shadowy groves of eucalyptus trees in a ghostly swirl of steam and iron laced by a shrill piping whistle.

Dubs 'B'

Moving now to the ostensibly similar B Class we find an engine which, although looking rather like the As, is quite a different proposition mechanically and historically. These were the first design by the N.C.R.'s famous Locomotive Superintendent D. A. Hendrie who, after the amalgamation of South Africa's railways in 1910, became C.M.E. of the S.A.R. from that year until 1922. More powerful than the As, these engines may be regarded as a cross between those and Reid's H Class, see page 109. All 25 came from the Dubs Workshops of the North British Locomotive Co., Glasgow, appearing in 1904, whereupon they undertook working the corridor trains from Durban. Under the S.A.R. these engines became classified 'G'.

It was to be 70 years later that we found two obsolescent engines lying in an overgrown siding at Witbank, their grimy attire transformed to gold by a low sun, making an exciting contrast with the conifers behind. Their future is uncertain for they are virtually the last remnants of the class and are the property of nearby Dunns Engineering Ltd.

Dunns is now world famous as the works which overhauls old steam locomotives for industrial use in South Africa. George Dunn, the founder, once worked for the Witbank Colliery Co. and when he left in 1946, Mr Hunter the present Colliery Engineer, see page 95, took over from him. He set up a small engineering concern in the centre of Witbank with both modest equipment and capital at his disposal. At that time the S.A.R. were repairing industrial locomotives and George Dunn took the opportunity to solicit this business by offering specialised attention and thenceforth progressed from strength to strength. After graduating to his present premises on the outskirts of Witbank a thriving company quickly developed and today his works yard can sometimes look like a 'Who's Who' of South African locomotive history. One of Dunn's most famous exploits was the purchase of a batch of 16th Class 2–8–2 + 2–8–2 Garratts from the Rhodesian Railways. These he overhauled and sold to collieries in the Transvaal, see page 155. Even today there appears to be a good future for this enterprising concern as South African industry is for ever requiring the more modern and powerful engines being cast aside by the S.A.R. and George Dunn acts as both mediator and refurbisher.

Leading Dimensions

	Improved Dubs 'A' 4–8–2T (S.A.R. A Class)	Dubs 'B' 4–8–2T (S.A.R. G Class)
Cylinders	17 in. × 21 in.	18 in. × 22 in.
Boiler pressure	160 lb per sq. in.	175 lb per sq. in.
Driving wheel diameter	3 ft 3 in.	3 ft 6 in.
Grate area	24 sq. ft	19 sq. ft
Tractive effort 75% b.p.	18,670 lb	22,280 lb
Total length	33½ ft	35½ ft
Total weight f.w.o.	50 tons 3 cwt	60 tons 6 cwt
Coal capacity	2¼ tons	2½ tons
Water capacity	1,358 gallons	1,560 gallons

Ex S.A.R. 'H2' 4–8–2T   Rear Endpaper

South Africa is a modern country and much of its industry developed during the present century. It is therefore inevitable that the country's locomotives should, in general, reflect this both mechanically and in appearance. Under such conditions a smattering of archaic-looking engines provides a vintage ring and few designs fulfil this function better than the H2 tanks. Not that they are exceptionally old – their relations the 'A's discussed on page 106 are older by 11 years, whilst quite a few other designs still extant in South Africa also precede them in time. The simple fact is that they look antiquated whilst, paradoxically, the Class A appears to be relatively modern! In fact the Hs were the larger successors to the As and when built possessed the interesting wheel arrangement of 4–10–2 as part of the Natal Government Railway's quest for more power in its 'all tank engine' policy. They were introduced for heavy duties over graded main lines, especially for the operation of coal traffic from Newcastle.

The first one came from Dubs in 1899 as a trial engine, having been designed by Reid of the Natal Government Railways and its success led to the construction of what was soon to become an important class totalling 101 engines. Additionally 35 Hs were built by Dubs/Neilson for the Imperial Military Railway during the Boer War. These engines later became the Central South African Railway's Class E. The engines were saturated and operated by slide valves. They held sway for some years as the N.G.R.'s crowning achievement in main line tanks until their inevitable replacement by larger tender engines; being ousted especially by Hendrie's 'B' 4–8–0s of 1904 (S.A.R. Class 1) – engines which today, along with the Hs, are relegated to industrial use only. After displacement from main line operation they graduated to shunting and secondary duties where their five-coupled wheels proved to be a disadvantage and they were converted to 4–8–2Ts by a simple removal of the rear pair of driving wheels. By 1911 most had been converted, becoming known as H2s, although the open horn gap in the framing, where the axle was removed, can still be seen today. After rebuilding some were later converted by the S.A.R. to 4–8–0s by subtracting the bunker and rear axle and adding a six-wheeled tender; these hybrids then became the S.A.R. Class 13. Others later ran as 4–8–0Ts + tender; such marrings being identical with those inflicted on the N.B. 4–8–2Ts mentioned on page 99. Over later years, under the S.A.R., many were sold to industry, whilst some were scrapped, but even as recently as 1970 a dozen or so H2s were still haunting the Durban Docks, being the last tank engines in main line service anywhere in South Africa.

The picture comes from Tavistock Colliery where three H2s have been given a green livery handsomely decked with red. Featured is Tavistock Colliery No. 2 named *Voortrekker*, an engine obtained second hand from the now dieselised I.S.C.O.R. – Iron & Steel Corporation, Pretoria. Above the smokebox can be seen her nameplate – this is beautifully curved with brass lettering and red backing. This particular design is my personal favourite, being similar to those once carried by the ex L.M.S. 'Jubilee' 4–6–0s.

Another of Tavistock's H2s, No. 3, is named *Flying Scotsman* and upon my naive assumption that it must commemorate either the famous British express train or the equally famous British pacific, I was greeted by a blank expression, for nothing so obvious had been the management's intention. Apparently it was a salute to a past engineer who was Scottish. The story went that this engineer was gifted with a remarkable agility as a sportsman and was such a force

110

to be reckoned with in the field that he acquired the nickname 'Flying Scotsman' from his rivals!

Actually, it will be seen that *Voortrekker* has cut-away tanks and a built-up bunker; these are recent innovations which tend to dissipate the antiquity of her lineation. The engines' duties at Tavistock are taking coals down to the electrified S.A.R. exchange at Kromklip some two miles distant and to see one of these curios easing a loaded train away from the colliery yard is a truly worthwhile experience. Fortunately an H type 4–10–2 is to be preserved, although this is a later engine, having been built in 1925 by North British to the original design at the specific request of the Witbank Colliery Co.

Original H Class 4–10–2T

No. built	Date	Builder
1	1899	Dubs & Co.
25	1901	Dubs & Co.
45	1902	Dubs & Co.
25	1903	Dubs & Co.
5	1903	North British

Leading Dimentions H2 Class 4–8–2T

Cylinders	19 in. $\times$ 27 in.
Boiler pressure	175 lb per sq. in.
Driving wheel diameter	3 ft 9 in.
Grate area	21 sq. ft
Tractive effort 85% b.p.	32,220 lb
Total length	$37\frac{1}{2}$ ft
Total weight f.w.o.	68 tons
Coal capacity	4 tons
Water capacity	1,880 gallons (non cut-away tank)

SOUTH AFRICAN GOLDFIELDS: Bagnall 4–8–2T industrial
Plate No. 18

Life is full of incongruities and much mental stimulation must derive from our various endeavours to make these coexistent. Imagine then, if you will, being caught in a traffic jam during the early morning rush hour in the prosperous gold mining town of Springs. The trappings of civilisation well up all around, sleek cars, chromium-plated shops with their abundance of sophisticated merchandise, towering blocks of offices, which a few decades ago belonged to fiction. Such images conjure up a sense of security; a complete society, the culmination of our traumatic past, for now we bask safely in its all-enveloping and protective façade. It seemed a shame that such perfection should be tarnished by the aberration of traffic jams, but paradoxically, it was possibly the cars themselves which added the greatest piquant to the aura of modernistic perfection which greeted me that morning.

Be this as it may, the comparison which met me on arrival at the engine shed of the South African Land Exploration Co. evoked a feeling of perplexity. Outside the old depot lay the remains of a period tank engine, whilst a sister engine was in the shed and, although out of sight, was well evidenced by virtue of steam thwacking noisily up into the depot roof. Suddenly, reality fell apart, the stage floor opened up, the scenery came crashing down and I fell bemused into the cellars of another age. Fifty years were retraced in an instant and, back in the 1920s, I beheld the leaking form of this Bagnall 4–8–2T as she issued herself clear from the shed portals. This period piece kindled vivid memories of Fowler's parallel-boilered 2300 2–6–4Ts, built for the London Midland & Scottish Railway from 1927 onwards. Like the 2300s she is heavily plated; observe the design's uncompromising parallels, then pass to the inclined cylinders, not forgetting the cab shaping and heavy bunker. There are many who would shudder at such comparisons, but however one equates it, these Bagnalls represent a glorious phase of past British industry.

The *Armadillo* as I named her on account of the heavy plating, was seized upon by a gang of Africans who proceeded to lavish her with water, coal and oil: the plenitude of labour being in itself more related to the days in which she originated. In no time at all the engine was ready to go and I barely had time to ascertain a destination from the driver. My hurried question solicited the fleeting and ambiguous reply, 'To the neck,' whereupon the engine glided away amid belching smoke and steam, leaving its moribund sister in even greater isolation, whilst we were left confronted by a mass of steaming earth and a heavily dripping water column.

Later that day, however, I was treated to a marvellous journey with the *Armadillo* from the Brakpan Gold Mines, H.Q. of the S.A.L.Ex.Co., to Reitfontein brickworks, a distance of 26 miles. The Company's railway linked Brakpan Mines with the S.A.R. at Springs but then continued through to Reitfontein serving other industry en route. We left Brakpan Mine with some loaded waggons for the S.A.R. connection at Springs after which we were to proceed light engined to Reitfontein to collect a trainload of bricks. Our African fireman industriously maintained boiler pressure and kept an immaculate footplate. At that time African firemen were not permitted on the main lines but were not infrequent on industrial locomotives. Musing over the single track which took us through the vast African township near Brakpan, the 4–8–2T seemed to be momentarily synonymous with its surroundings, but as we passed through the suburbs of Springs with its ultra-modern dwellings and their exquisitely cultured gardens our engine became once again a haunting phantom, a blemish tolerated only by the courtesy of industrial necessity and even that ill-attended to by the technology of the age.

After leaving Springs we passed through derelict gold mines rife with atmosphere. On both sides of the line fallen structures of bleached and crumbling brickwork were painfully straining to reach above the vegetation which continually threatened them with annihilation. Eventually we passed into open country and still this strange engine evoked images: this time of a Fowler 2300 clanking its way across the old branch line from Leicester to Rugby, for this was a scene I remember well from my childhood – a time when these engines held sway on such services in Britain. Possibly it was also the embankments we crossed which additionally characterised the Leicester to Rugby line as did the steady rattling pace of our progress. Our pause at Reitfontein afforded further inspection and I noticed, in very marked contrast with the 2300s, how small her driving wheels were whilst a more surprising aspect of this phenomenon was the remarkable similarity in size between them and her bogie wheels.

The engine was one of a number built by Bagnall of Stafford for South African industry during the 1930s. Another engine of identical type was, until recently, to be found at the East Daggafontein Gold Mine, another haven of steam traction. But these have now passed into history leaving the *Armadillo* as the last active survivor of her type.

Ex LMS Fowler 2300 2–6–4T 1927

Leading Dimentions

Cylinders	16 in. × 24 in.
Boiler pressure	180 lb per sq. in.
Driving wheel diameter	3 ft 3 in.
Grate area	17 sq. ft
Tractive effort 85% b.p.	24,103 lb
Total length	36½ ft
Total weight f.w.o.	58 tons
Coal capacity	3½ tons
Water capacity	1,500 gallons

SOUTH AFRICAN GOLDFIELDS: Western Holdings North British 4-8-2T 18 in.
Plate No. 34

I was afforded a pleasant interlude at Welkom in the Orange Free State when, after taking a brief repose from the bustling activities of the nearby Kroonstad–Bloemfontein main line, I visited the Western Holdings Gold concern to film their delightful little N.B. 4–8–2T. She is one of a widely assorted range of locomotives which inhabit South Africa's famous 'golden arc'. This is the name given to the 330-mile-long curve of the Republic's gold fields. Welkom is situated near the southern tip as the field extends from Virginia, in the Orange Free State, through the Transvaal via Klerksdorp and Johannesburg to Kinross. The mines of this belt are working the most extensive and consistent deposits of gold-bearing ore ever discovered and the towns of Germiston, Springs and Johannesburg, along with many others, are world famous for their gold industry; some half a million people are employed on workings throughout the arc. Much of this region is characterised by the enormous heaps of stone waste which loom up intermittently like giant pyramids above the flat landscape, whilst the decoratively coloured winding gear situated above the shafts along with their concomitant outbuildings are an equally specific aspect of the region. South Africa has been richly blessed by nature with many valuable minerals, for she industriously mines diamonds, platinum, chrome, coal, iron, manganese and uranium in addition to gold, but it is the coal and gold fields which are host to the steam locomotive.

The Western Holdings concern is owned by Anglo American and the mine at Welkom has four shafts in operation. Usually the steam engines only work between No. 2 shaft and the reduction plant, as No. 3 shaft is operated by a rather ugly Maffei-built diesel, No. 4 shaft dispenses its ore underground, whilst No. 1 shaft is situated alongside the reduction plant itself, thus allowing the ore to be fed in by conveyor belt.

The Company has two other steam engines at the mine, both standard North British 4–8–2Ts in original condition, as discussed on page 97. The engine illustrated, however, is much smaller than these standards, being neater in appearance and possibly daintier – if such an adjective befits an engine! A locomotive of fascinating personality, she is North British No. 24660, built in 1940. Her overall style is not completely dissimilar to her larger relations and a comparison of dimensions might be made between those below and the ones on page 100. Western Holdings obtained this engine from Brakpan Mines in 1962 for a sum of 15,000 Rand.

She is seen in action trundling a loaded ore train up from No. 2 shaft on a bitterly cold winter's night at a time when a world shortage of gold necessitated extensive operations and high production. The gold ore is dramatically silhouetted against the night sky with which it makes a pleasing contrast, as indeed does the engine set against its rake of pallid hopper waggons.

Leading Dimensions

Cylinders	18 in. × 22 in.
Boiler pressure	180 lb per sq. in.
Driving wheel diameter	3 ft 6 in.
Grate area	$17\frac{1}{4}$ sq. ft
Total heating surface	1,195 sq. ft
Coal capacity	$4\frac{1}{4}$ tons
Water capacity	1,560 gallons

S.A.R. 15F/23 Class 4–8–2   **Plates Nos. 1, 9, 20, 43**

Fulfilling a long cherished dream, I at last beheld the gleaming metals of the Kroonstad–Bloemfontein line – possibly the busiest steam-worked line in the world and operated entirely by the impressive 15F/23 Class 4–8–2s. Imagine my elation – for on busy days this route is traversed by one hundred steam trains – many double-headed! There are few railway lovers who would not equate this with the now mourned days of epic steam in their homelands, whilst those of younger years would experience, if only once, the magic offered by an intensely worked steam railway in its full fling. I was at Theunisson, a large intermediate station situated just south of the ever-encroaching electrification caternary which was spreading like a cancer across this paradise.

No sooner had I reached the line than the vermilion-coloured semaphores flicked almost secretively upwards against the blue sky signalling a train. Like a child I was impatient for the oncoming train, oblivious of my surroundings, and keyed up for the first sight of the locomotive. After feverishly scanning the veld I eventually spotted its lightly-sooted smoke trail. A chime whistle cried out and the ground trembled as a 15F swung into view with a dust trail blowing up alongside her speeding train. With another long sonorous cry the mighty 4–8–2 lunged through the station, her driving wheels spinning in a shimmering tapestry of movement. A warm sooty haze momentarily engulfed me, soon to be blown away by the waggons dancing and bustling their way behind the engine. As the last waggons finally swirled by, a sheet of newspaper gently settled earthwards and balls of tumbleweed, having leapt in ecstasy during the affray, rolled to rest and resumed their slumbers around the goods yard: the wind having long since deposited them there from the surrounding countryside.

Unbelievably, the pegs were immediately off for the other direction and two minutes later another chime whistle sounded, heralding the approach of 23 Class *Kroonstad* on a south-bound special passenger. As she throbbed through the station with a 17-coach express made up of red and cream clerestory coaches, the entire building shook, the newspaper once again lifted by her 'slipstream'. My mind transformed the scene to an A4 Pacific racing through Grantham – an illusion aided by the screaming swish of coaching stock; the visitor to South Africa will inevitably superimpose his own distant recollections onto such incidents.

Reborn, revitalised and revisited by something very close to me, I continued to enjoy the fascination offered by this wonderful railway. During this time I came upon Vetrivier, an important watering and fire tending stop, lying approximately half way, being situated 69 miles south of Kroonstad on this 116-mile route. Here are placed several lines for each direction, each provided with an overhead water crane along with deep pits between tracks to facilitate fire raking – these pits are situated slightly ahead of the water columns to enable both operations to be executed simultaneously. The water supply is pumped from the adjacent river by Theunisson Council, going initially into three reservoirs situated on a nearby koppie. From there it passes under high pressure to a large tank at either end of the station as depicted by plate 9. These tanks hold 40,000 gallons. Two Africans are permanently engaged at either end of the station to assist in watering and also to convey ash from the pits by wheelbarrow to waggons in adjacent sidings.

Upon my arrival a double-headed freight was in at the north end with a 15F and 23 and, fascinated, I watched the servicing operations. It is quite commonplace to incorporate fire raking stops on South African main lines. Although this practice is unknown on many railways one must consider that S.A.R. engines work incredibly hard, often on coal which has a tendency to clog up when burnt. Exactly how hard these engines operate can be ably demonstrated by the deep layer of cinders, sometimes well over a foot thick which lie at the tracksides: often as far as 40 feet from the railway one can still measure them several inches deep! More eloquent testimony could hardly be given, and one is reminded of the heroic saga on the old London & North Western Railway when the steady pattering of cinders cascading downwards onto carriage roofs was a commonplace characteristic of travel.

Watching the two giants, I noticed an African cycling alongside the metals from the direction of the station and as he drew up to me his bike wobbled to a stop and inclining his head in my direction he slowly drawled the accost, 'The baws wants to see you, suh.' The boss was the Vetrivier station master and once assured that I agreed to go to see him, my new acquaintance, satisfied that his duty was done, promptly turned his bike round and pedalled precariously back towards base in a manner not unreminiscent of a moving crab – cycling alongside a railway is not the easiest method of transportation! I feared that this summons might herald a challenge to my presence, for although I had authority to be there, perhaps I was not welcome. After being temporarily mesmerised by the two departing 4–8–2s, I made my way to the station in answer to my summons and to await whatever fate might befall me. I hurried because already the pegs were off in both directions as more trains approached this unbelievably busy crossing and I was determined not to miss any. My fears were groundless, for on reaching the office a cherry 'Hello, you're from England,' greeted me. He quickly explained that he knew I was in the area and was anxious that I should not pass by without seeing him and, fearing that I might quit Vetrivier before he found such opportunity, had promptly sent his messenger boy to me the moment I had been noticed on the bank.

'You could do with some tea,' my friend informed me as he busily filled a small kettle and, as three cups and saucers were ceremoniously rattled into order, he enquired what he might tell me about Vetrivier and its locomotives.

That afternoon passed in conversation, first upon this now famous stretch of railway, thence to the 4–8–2s themselves. 'Do you know,' he proudly announced, 'that these locomotives take 15 million gallons of water per month from here? The equivalent of one day's consumption for the entire city of Bloemfontein!' Staggering though these figures are, they may be easily substantiated by an average of 130 engines per 24 hours – possibly only 90 trains but many double-headed – each engine taking an average 4,000 gallons. The 15F and 23 tenders hold some 6,000 and 9,000 gallons respectively but these would not be empty upon reaching Vetrivier. This figure, over a 30-day period does indeed total 15 million, albeit based on my own rough calculations. A 4–8–2 is reckoned to use about 100 gallons of water per mile and accordingly, on the run up from Bloemfontein, the 15Fs have to take water at Glen, whilst the 23s with their much bigger tenders can easily reach Vetrivier without replenishment. The cost of this water is 2,500 Rand per month! Add to this the equally amazing statistic that 1,400 tons of ash is shovelled out of Vetrivier's pits monthly, this being sent to Natal for road construction.

One 4–8–2 can take some 1,250 tons over this route, a brace handling over 2,000 tons. Certainly these loads are not unduly excessive but the track is very undulating with many adverse gradients. Furthermore traffic has to be kept moving at more than a trot and indeed sometimes the trains are whipped up to very sprightly paces. Going northwards the trains often consist of coal empties returning to Witbank, fruit and imports from the Cape, sheep from the Karroo and cars from the big factories around Port Elizabeth, whilst southwards go trainloads of Witbank coal, grain from the northern agricultural regions and general industrial traffic from the Transvaal. Additionally the Durban–Johannesburg petrol pipeline is intercepted at Kroonstad and petrol for the south thence proceeds by rail. I conferred my knowledge of the forthcoming electrification to my friend and in reply he sadly informed me that this was expected to be in operation sometime in 1975/6.

Is any steam engine in the world today more modern looking than these 4–8–2s? Personally I doubt that any steam locomotive can look truly modern in 1974 so conditioned must we be to the totally different visual aspects of modern technology, but I would hand the laurels to these engines as readily as to any other, even though their basic design was prepared some fifty years ago. The 15Fs may be traced back to 1935 when A. G. Watson, the South African Railways' C.M.E., produced a batch of 36 engines which were an enlarged version of the 15CAs, page 89, but having the Rotary Cam Valve Gear fashionable at that time. These were known as the 15Es. From 1938 onwards, building of the type continued under Watson's successor W. A. Day, but these later engines possessed Walschaerts Valve Gear instead of the Rotary Cams and so were born the 15Fs – which were destined to become the most numerous steam class on the African Continent eventually totalling 255 engines. Originally they were built for hand firing, but provision was made for conversion to mechanical stoking and today most are mechanically operated. That the 15Fs are based on the 15CA is dramatically shown when one is seen minus its smoke deflectors – an addition which greatly blurs the origins of the design.

The 23s appeared simultaneously as a new 4–8–2 design by Day, the first also entering service in 1938. Originally, these were intended to have 5 ft 6 in. driving wheels as part way between the 5 ft 0 in. 15Fs and 6 ft 0 in. 16E Pacifics, but this would have involved designing a new boiler. The outbreak of war was already feared and as the engines were urgently needed, no time was taken to design a new boiler and a compromise situation was reached whereby the standard 3B-type boiler of a 15F was used and the driving wheels cast at 5 ft 3 in. diameter. The extra boiler length was then taken up by the smokebox. As it happened the last 23s were delivered from Germany just before World War II broke out. To compensate for a larger driving wheel diameter, the boiler pressure was increased to 225 lb per sq. in., bringing the tractive effort comparable with the 15Fs. The 23s were put to work over the Karroo desert, hence their immense 9,500 gallon tenders, and their total of 136 engines when added to the 15Fs has formed the backbone of the S.A.R.'s steam fleet ever since. They have operated over much of the Republic and even today are still widely distributed. Almost identical in looks, it has always been something of a test to distinguish the classes apart – excepting, of course, the 23s' ultra-long tenders. This has recently developed into a more difficult task as some 15Fs have become attached to 23 type tenders! Otherwise, the main visible differences are in the driving wheel diameter, which, although only 3 in. larger on a 23, is quite noticeable; their chimneys also being larger than the scaled-down ones on the 15Fs.

Prior to my leaving Vetrivier my friend had arranged for me to meet Charlie Lewis, the well known railway photographer who was the part author of *Steam on the Veld*. One day later I arrived at Charlie's house in Bloemfontein to be greeted by a group of eminent enthusiasts including Charlie's wife and Chris Butcher from the Rhodesian Railways. Within minutes I was confronted with home-made cakes, lashings of coffee and as voluminous an assortment of railway literature as it had ever been my pleasure to witness. Although both Charlie and Chris knew Britain well, the evening's conversation did not dwell on the moribund history of British steam, for we aspired to greener pastures by discussing in animated tones the splendours of African steam in the 1970s and instead of tedious and often hackneyed reminiscences, our conversation glittered with the liveliness of a glorious present. Sedentary enthusiasts might pessimistically acclaim that, 'It is alright for some,' but steam is still a living force in the world, its magnificent spirit undiminished, albeit that one now has to travel further than hitherto. We were into the early hours before our meeting broke up but not before firm arrangements had been made for us all to reassemble shortly after dawn on the koppie at Karree which overlooks the most famous railway photographic spot in South Africa – a sharp curve on the 9-mile climb at 1 in 100 up from Glen, some miles to the north of Bloemfontein on the Kroonstad main line.

As I hoped, the morning sun rose into a cloudless sky and within half an hour of sunrise I was to be found driving along the rough track which led to the celebrated koppie. A vehicle which I assumed to belong to Charlie and Chris had already been parked alongside, but on reaching the mound's photographic side my assumption proved to be wrong, as two South African photographers, unknown to me, were busily setting up tripods. A double-headed freight was already on the climb pumping dual exhaust columns into the frosty air and the spectacle was greeted by a healthy clicking of shutters as two 15Fs roared by in epic fashion, their deep-throated exhausts bellowing across the surrounding veld. There was still no sign of the others by the time 23 Class *City of Pretoria* slogged northwards with a heavy passenger train and, in fact, the sun was well up before my companions arrived, having been delayed by a puncture. We immediately told them what pictures we had made, but Charlie disregarded these as a millionaire might disregard a penny, for Bloemfontein and its 4–8–2s were an everyday part of his life. He knew Karree as a second home, and well I ought to have realised it for, to him, even a dawn meeting there had more than a shade of social overtones.

The light remained good for another hour or two, and the non-ending procession of 4–8–2s thenceforth received even fuller justice from the augmented battery of cameras now situated on the koppie. Charlie told us of the great mornings he had known at Karree, when, after exceptionally heavy frost, the exhaust trails seemed to freeze in the air above the trains, echoing the curvature of the line. On such days it was sometimes possible to count exhausts from seven different trains! By mid-morning the sun had rolled too far over and we quit the location. So ended my time on the world's busiest steam main line and although I bade farewell to Charlie, plans were already under way for me to join up with Chris Butcher in Rhodesia at a later date.

15F Building Sequence			*23 Building Sequence*		
S.A.R. No.	*Builder*	*Date*	*S.A.R. No.*	*Builder*	*Date*
2902–8	Schwartzkopf	1938	2552–8	Schwartzkopf	1938
2909–22	Henschel	1938	2559–71	Henschel	1938
2923–66	N. British	1939	3201–85	Henschel	1938
2967–96	Beyer Peacock	1944	3286–3316	Schwartzkopf	1939
2997–3056	N. British	1944		(Total 136.)	
3057–3156	N. British	1948	to World War II)		
	(Total 255)				

	15F	*23*
	Leading Dimensions	*Leading Dimensions*
Cylinders	24 in. × 28 in.	24 in. × 28 in.
Boiler pressure	210 lb per sq. in.	225 lb per sq. in.
Driving wheel diameter	5 ft 0 in.	5 ft 3 in.
Grate area	63 sq. ft	63 sq. ft
Tractive effort 85% b.p.	47,980 lb	48,960 lb
Total length	73½ ft	87 ft 3 in.
Total weight f.w.o.	178 tons approx.	219 tons approx.
Coal capacity	14 tons	18 tons
Water capacity	6,000 gallons	9,500 gallons

S.A.R. Class 25NC 4–8–4   **Plate No. 8**

Along with their condensing sisters the 25s, these magnificent machines represent the ultimate in S.A.R. steam design and were the final main line steam engines delivered to South Africa. Apart from the condensing apparatus they are identical with the 25s, separately discussed on page 125.

To meet increased traffic requirements on S.A.R. main lines in the early 1950s it became necessary to provide further large locomotives of a more sophisticated design than the 15F/23 4–8–2s. It was decided to incorporate the best qualities of the 15F/23s but with an improved boiler design and other enhanced features. Extensive tests were conducted on Class 23 locomotives with modified boilers, to determine the best design and to glean the most efficient steaming performance, but without any radical departure from normal construction. However, this gave the new engines a combustion chamber, allowing the tubes to be decreased in length to 19 ft, as against 22½ ft on the 4–8–2s. A 4–8–4 wheel arrangement for the engine and two six-wheel bogies for the tender were decided upon after considerations regarding weight distribution; the new engines were classified 25. In order to increase availability, roller bearings were fitted to all side rods and wheels, as locomotives possessing traditional types of motion and axlebox bearings frequently required attention between shopping. Thus it was anticipated that, except for lubrication of the roller bearings, no attention to these aspects of 25 Class engines would ever be required by running sheds. The engine frame, cylinders, trailing bogie, leading bogie, tender frame and tender bogies were all of cast steel and manufactured in the USA and it was intended that repairs to these would be considerably less than to the fabricated types. The locomotive frame and cylinders were cast in one piece.

Originally it was intended to obtain locomotives with conventional tenders only. However, due to the ever-increasing seriousness of water shortages, especially in the Karroo, the S.A.R. decided to have some condensing engines as well. Accordingly 90 condensing locomotives and 50 non-condensing ones were ordered, the latter known as 25NC.

Most 25NCs are allocated to the important railway junction of De Aar from which they work up the main line to Kimberley. At De Aar they come under the responsibility of the Locomotive Foreman, A. G. Watson, a man known throughout the world for the pride he has built up in locomotive operations at this important depot. Before Mr Watson took over at De Aar, engines were filthy and most operations there were regarded merely as a job of work, but this inveterate enthusiast soon injected a new spirit. He began by cleaning up all his shunting engines, simultaneously forbidding the crews either to slip them or to emit heavy smoke; any driver contravening these orders was hauled up onto the carpet. Commensurate with this, he named one shunting engine, a 15AR 4–8–2, *Prudence*. From these beginnings Gordon Watson turned to the main liners introducing a policy of one man, one engine, and today 35 De Aar engines have their own drivers – only three of his 34 25NC Class belong to the pool, the remainder all being assigned. Needless to say, cleanliness is now a general rule, the men love their engines, many spending much time polishing them whilst, furthermore, this old-time pride permeates throughout the entire depot; the shed staff keeping the engines basically clean with the drivers looking after all finer points: many cab interiors have to be seen to be believed!

Another Watson innovation is the introduction of numbers onto buffer beams by way of attractively cast numerals, but perhaps his master touch is the naming of his 25NCs, engines which he personally loves a great deal – a marked contrast to his feelings about the 25s. He bestowed them all with girls' names, choosing many personally, but some commemorated the names of the drivers' wives. I asked him why he chose to name such giants after girls and herein lay yet another master touch, 'Because,' he added with a wink of maturity, 'it takes men to control them!' Could the sages themselves have made a more discerning comment? Here are their names:

3401	*Anne*	3413	*Trudie*	3425	*Trixie*
3402	*Alice*	3414	*Carol*	3426	*Delise*
3403	*Joyce*	3415	*Zelda*	3427	*Ina*
3404	*Heidi*	3416	*Elma*	3428	*Ezette*
3405	*Topsy*	3417	*Susanna*	3429	*Jennifer*
3406	*Ilise*	3418	*Jessie*	3430	*Sharon*
3407	*Louise*	3419	*Estelle*	3431	*Lindy-Lou*
3408	*Esther*	3420	*Patricia*	3432	*Lady Jane*
3409	*Charlotte*	3421	*Erika*	3433	*Heather*
3410	*Gillian*	3422	*Fiona*	3434	*Corry*
3411	*Olga*	3423	*Victoria*		
3412	*Harriet*	3424	*Marjorie*		

Their names are carried on rectangular plates affixed to the engine smokebox.

On the Kimberley road at the fire and water stop at Orangeriver it is common to see drivers vigorously polishing their already spotless engines whilst servicings are carried out – a story goes around De Aar that some men love their engines more than their wives! The crews leave all their personal kit on the engines except when they go away to shops then, of course, everything, including nameplates and all adornments, has to be removed. Today, Mr Watson is operating the same mileage with 62 engines as the depot was operating with 83 when he took over in 1970! Southwards from Kimberley the main line continues, over the Karroo, to Beaufort West – this stretch being principally worked by the latter depot's 25s. Mr Watson shows little interest in the condensing giants which infiltrate his domain and many De Aar drivers shun the prospect of having a 25 as pilot engine when double-heading; so great a mess do they make of the spotless 25NCs, the condensers are regarded as the S.A.R.'s smuttiest and smokiest engines – no mean claim indeed!

De Aar depot, apart from its gleaming array of power, is also considerably enlivened by Mr Watson's museum which he personally administrates on behalf of the S.A.R. The shed apprentices restore the old engines before they pass them for static preservation to nearby tracks specially laid for the purpose. Already Mr Watson has assembled representatives of classes 6A, 6B, 16E, GDA, GL, 4AR and 15A with many others scheduled to appear in the future.

It was a very real pleasure to meet this dedicated man who made me so welcome at De Aar, for quite apart from keeping control of all operations at this depot, he also finds time to enthuse about his engines' characters and performances. As he showed me around, he was anxious that I should not miss *Karen*, a 15AR done out in an idyllic shade of deep violet – and what a beautiful contrast she made with the towering 4–8–4s which beshadowed her on all sides. A delicious 12A named *Stephanie* was flirting her way around on station pilot duties with much pomp and circumstance, showing off her highly polished exterior and beautifully curved nameplate to anyone who would afford her an eye.

If I am permitted to make just one last analogy with the halcyon days of British steam I would claim the greatest railway thrill of my life to have been a visit to Crewe North engine sheds where lines of giant steam locomotives were tightly packed side by side – Duchesses, Princess Royals and Britannias. What an atmosphere of power and majesty that depot had! The mind clings passionately to such precious memories though they are of events long past, but when I saw the rows of gleaming 25 and 25NC 4–8–4s and 23 Class 4–8–2s in the great depot at Kimberley, I was confronted by a spectacle which matched the marvellous memories of Crewe. The aroma, the intense presence, the pent-up pressure and the sheer awesome power of giant engines signified this deeply thrilling encounter. In the yard a spotless 25NC named *City of East London*, by ornate nameplates on her smoke deflectors, represented one of the world's last great steam achievements. On a nearby road stood *Worcester*, another 25NC. These are the 'Duchesses' of the 1970s, as the 23s are the 'Britannias'.

Building Sequence

S.A.R. No.	Builder	Date
3401–11	North British	1953
3412–50	Henschel	1953

Leading Dimensions

Cylinders	24 in. × 28 in.
Boiler pressure	225 lb per sq. in.
Driving wheel diameter	5 ft 0 in.
Grate area	70 sq. ft
Tractive effort 85% b.p.	51,410 lb
Total weight f.w.o.	213 tons
Total length	91½ ft
Coal capacity	18 tons (mechanically stoked)
Water capacity	10,500 gallons

S.A.R. Class 25 'Condenser' 4–8–4   Plates Nos. 3, 21, 36, 41, 45

Mr Watson welcomed us to his home and promptly ushered us into a delightful room whose walls were decked with locomotive pictures, many of considerable interest; I feasted upon this unexpected gallery. 'Must we really spend the evening discussing Condensers?' Mr Watson sighed, 'You know I don't like them. Might we not discuss the merits of Hornby modelling instead?' I firmly declined any such capitulation by emphasising that the 25s were the highlight of my 7,000-mile journey and that furthermore, they may soon be withdrawn – this latter point being emphasised by none other than our host earlier that day!

Conscience won the day. The depot chief sat back in his chair in a manner befitting one about to undergo interrogation and said, 'Did you know that we have always had trouble obtaining suitable water supplies in the Karroo, especially between Touws River and Beaufort

West but also between Beaufort West and De Aar?' My affirmation prompted him to continue. 'Many years ago there was talk of converting some 12As into condensers but this did not materialise and it was not until 1949 that we obtained our first condensing tender from Henschel of Germany. We attached this to the Class 20 2–10–2 – I don't suppose you would know about her, she was broken up years ago! In this condition the 20 could run some 600 miles without needing water replenishment and I think it was the all round success of this engine which finally convinced the management to go in for some condensing locomotives. Henschel were pioneers with condensing engines, sending them to the Argentine, Iraq and Russia and I remember during the last war Henschel developed some condensing tenders for Hitler's war engines as part of their attempted Russian conquest.' I recalled reading about the renowned German 2–10–0s.

Continuing his tale, Mr Watson soon forgot his prejudices and began to explain, with some animation how the 25s worked. 'The exhaust steam is fed into a turbine driving a fan blower in order to eject gases out of the smokebox – can't spare any steam for jobs like that!' he said. 'Then the exhaust passes through the huge 16 in. diameter pipe, which is visible on the engine's left-hand side, before going through an oil separator and then through another turbine which drives five air intake fans situated in the tender top, before finally passing to steam condensing elements mounted on both sides of the tender.' My assumption that the fans provided cool air by drawing it in from the atmosphere via the meshing on the tender sides whilst simultaneously ejecting warm air through the tender top proved to be correct, our host only adding that the fans are individually driven by bevel gear on a lone shaft from the fan turbine. 'The steam cascades into water,' he continued, 'and the condensate is collected in a tank slung beneath the tender frame in readiness for refeeding into the engine's boiler. I think possibly one of their most ingenious tricks is the setting of one safety valve at slightly below maximum permissible boiler pressure and discharging it into the 16 in. pipe to be condensed!'

At this juncture Mr Watson rose and crossed the room to a small bureau from which he extracted a leaflet entitled *Henschel Condensing Locomotives*. 'This gives the principal points,' he announced. 'This is Henschel's official catalogue – it says the 25s are the largest condensers ever built!' From this he read as follows:

(a) The Henschel condensing locomotive is an orthodox type of engine, the only difference being that the exhaust steam from the cylinder is not blown into the atmosphere but conveyed to the tender where it is condensed in an air cooling system.

(b) Distances of up to 700 miles can be covered without replenishing water. These locomotives are especially suitable for service in arid regions or in regions with unfavourable feed water.

(c) The saving in water compared with the non-condensing locomotive amounts to approximately 90%.

(d) Feeding the boiler with condensate – only 10% of fresh water being added – results in a corresponding longer boiler life.

(e) A saving in fuel is attained as the boiler is fed with hot condensate.

(f) The power for the condensing system and the draught fan is obtained from the energy of the exhaust steam practically without detraction from the locomotive's output.

(g) The condensing equipment requires no special attention from the crew.

'There', said out friend, 'that's everything you want to know.' 'What were you saying this afternoon about their frames being in one casting?' I enquired with rapidly increasing interest. Mr Watson replied, 'The engines' frames are a one-piece steel casting with the cylinders cast integrally having come from the General Steel Casting Corporation, USA. Making the frames in this manner has the advantage that numerous separate parts such as cylinders, cylinder covers, buffer beams, drag boxes, cross stays, pivot castings and boiler support brackets, etc., are eliminated and there is therefore no danger of them working loose. Thus it was intended that a large amount of repair work normally connected with such parts would be dispensed with and this has in fact been the case. Of course in these respects the 25NC engines are identical.'

'Once they were in action,' our host persevered, 'the 25s certainly proved their merit and became an economical proposition even though they cost some £112,000 each compared with about £70,000 for a 25NC – and that was in 1953! Their introduction enabled closure of some Karroo watering stations and dispensed with the need to transport water into the desert during the dry season. This, as you will imagine, was a very costly business. They have always been a good free-running engine having roller bearings throughout, the Skefko type on all axles, but nineteen of the Class have Timpken ones on their coupling rods. Nowadays the entire class have split crosshead bars. There is a story of one which blew away during a gale at Cape Town – so relatively small is the effort required to move them! This particular

127

90 Condensing Locomotives for South Africa

The latest of a long line of locomotives supplied by the North British Locomotive Company to South Africa railways is the Class 25 condensing type of locomotive, illustrated above.

Orders for ninety of these locomotives and thirty condensing tenders were placed with this Company in 1951 by the South African Railways and Harbours Administration, in addition to ten Class 25 NC non-condensing 4-8-4 type locomotives.

Over a hundred years' experience and skill goes into the building of every North British locomotive. The traditional craftsmanship of the Scottish Engineers allied to the progressive spirit of the management has kept this Company abreast of every modern development.

These and many other factors have placed the North British Locomotive Company in the forefront of the world's Steam, Diesel Hydraulic and Electric Locomotive Builders.

SERVING THE RAILWAYS OF THE WORLD

engine, which was dead at the time, suddenly began to move away. Fortunately it was noticed by the depot foreman who chased after it and stopped it by throwing chunks of wood under the wheels!

'We have had a few bizarre incidents with them, as one would expect from such unconventional machines. First was the trouble with the exhaust fans through char cutting them, whilst at first the fan bearings could not tolerate the heat. Originally the fans would not blow the char out so we evolved the pear-shaped front whereby all char fell into the bottom of the neck, then by fitting a steam ejector into this neck the char was successfully exhausted. But they are dirty engines to work on – try riding behind one in the first coach, you will be as black as the crew. In fact we don't like using them on passenger trains for these very reasons!'

'Tell them about the incident at Reims,' said Mrs Watson, who had by this time joined our circle. 'You mean the one which blew its chimney out?' retorted her husband. 'Yes, that was caused by the exhaust fan breaking loose and blowing off the complete chimney structure – that chimney lay on Reims station for years afterwards. Then, on another occasion, the fan broke through an engine's tube-plate causing water and steam, at full boiler pressure, to shoot out of the chimney – just like a geyser. Numerous tender fans have broken loose too, usually when the engine is moving; they break away from the tender housing and fly off up into the air. I will never forget the time when this happened to one of my men and his subsequent report of seeing what he took to be a helicopter following his train, before realising, to his horror, that one of the tender fans had gone. There are several of them lying about the Karroo should you want to examine one,' Mr Watson smilingly said. 'Wait till you see one going along with its tender puffing,' he continued, 'they look so ridiculous. Nowadays many of the tenders are in such poor condition that the leaks cause them to puff in accord with the engine's exhaust beats – exactly as does the chimney of a conventional engine!'

At this moment Mr Watson's daughter brought in a large pot of coffee. 'Still discussing the Camels, are you?' she asked, placing the tray before us. 'I was just telling them about the puffing tenders', replied Mr Watson. 'Yes, those engines create quite a lot of interest, but they're quite the filthiest things on the railway', she opined. Our host continued, 'They may not work for much longer as the stretch they were really built for between Touws River and Beaufort West is now electrified and the water problem between De Aar and Beaufort is largely overcome. I don't know why they didn't convert them years ago. Did you know that No. 3468 is now in Salt River Works being converted to a non-condensing engine; whether she will create a precedent for the entire class is not known – I have heard that after the forthcoming dieselisation programme they may break them up completely.' I suggested that the 25s might be retained as main line engines elsewhere in the Republic but my informant insisted, 'Not in their present state – maintenance is a big problem even to us who know them well. Just think, there are the turbine fans to maintain, expensive pumps for feeding hot condensate into the boiler – because, don't forget, the temperature of the feed water is far too high to use ordinary injectors. Then the condensing tenders are very expensive to maintain in efficient working order, especially now they are getting old; with their condensing elements, fans and other paraphernalia – I much prefer the 25NCs any day!'

Thenceforth I yielded that the 25NCs, of which our host was justifiably proud, should predominate over the remainder of the evening's conversation. Upon leaving the Watson's that evening we swung southwards towards the Karroo. For him the occasion had been routine enough, but for me it had set into motion one of the greatest love affairs of my life.

Later that night I was to experience one of the first fruits of this affair – the thrill of hearing a condenser at speed. It was from a small lineside hotel situated on the periphery of the Karroo; the occasion was one I will never forget. It was a Saturday and, as is customary in many South African hotels at this time, a small band was in residence, their endeavours being audible from my room, and it was with relief on my part that they took an interval prior to playing their final set. When the band stopped everything seemed strangely quiet, save for the tinkling of glasses and an occasional murmur of voices from the ballroom. An owl called, his cry piercing the night, until after a few minutes he too fell silent, presumably having moved on to richer pastures than the hotel environs offered. A spell of quietness was broken by some terrestrial disturbance, a slight shudder convulsed the building, followed by a deep rumbling above which could be heard a whine like a jet aircraft. It came ever closer as if a mighty whirlwind was about to engulf the hotel and dash it to the ground, demolishing it to a mass of smithereens. The cacophony gushed to a climax as a 25 howled through, the fearsome scream of its fans riding high above the roar of speeding waggons. After the train had passed and normality gathered together its shattered fragments, the little band struck up again almost as if they had waited to pay homage to the fading sounds of the condenser. As they launched merrily into the 32 bars of a 1930s pop number, the ringing banjo rose above the heavier brass and percussion, seeming, as it did so, to mimic the way in which a 25's turbine rides above the sound of a heavy train. The band was to continue for some time, but I was unaware of it because, like every locomotive lover I have ever met, there are few things more conducive to rest than days spent with enormous steam engines. I learned later that the owl outlived all the evening's activity and continued his nocturnal enterprises from an unknown vantage point.

How does one describe the wild Karroo? A place where warm, sunny days are separated from cold, inky nights by a twilight drama of black hills and purple sunsets. A treeless and stunted expanse; paradise of the Aardvark, Rock Dassie, Cape Raven and Pied Crow to begin an endless succession. Throughout the frost-tinged winter days the pure blue skies are seldom interrupted by anything other than the musty umber of locomotive smoke which hangs between the golden hills like a gathering stormcloud and, of all wild places, this seemingly uninhabited expanse harbours a million searching eyes. Was not this steam's last fling in the great landscape of the world?

Under mesmerisation, if not actually obsession, I endeavoured to put onto film the condensers' dynamic individuality; an individuality so pungent as frequently to overshadow the desert atmosphere. Thus I played my key contribution in the love affair: plate 45 symbolises an aspect of delicious crudity; plate 36 sets one amid the barren, inhospitable terrain to which they owe their creation whilst, in contrast, plate 21 shows one bathed in evening sunlight demurely whirring its merchandise back on to the main line after being looped. On plate 3 we see one at high speed with an express perishables train storming across the desert against the semaphores which colourfully tinge the environment and characterise the essentiality of the engine's setting. Look at her ugly, jutting, questioning, pear drop-shaped smokebox! But it is plate 41 which really epitomises my feelings for these engines. I have titled this picture in the nomenclature of Turner by calling it 'Eruption: two condensers ease up to the semaphores with fires made up and blow down valves screaming'. When I saw these two struggling to get their train under way, I could scarcely believe my eyes. I was almost too stunned to control my camera. What affliction racked my frame to produce such effect? This was their

131

'magnum opus', and my crowning fortune, because I was able to capture that ephemeral instant which to me characterised them so completely. Such romanticism in pictorialism may be justified in that it is a liberty of art, as indeed of much human action, to be chimerical.

Many trains were double-headed, one 25 being allowed some 1,800 tons, whilst two handled something less than 3,000 tons. The double-headers were magnificent; imagine 216 ft of locomotive and over 100,000 lb of tractive effort (85% b.p.) on one train. Do not be misled by the 3 ft 6 in. gauge, for not only are South African engines built to within 3 in. of the British loading gauge, they are permitted to be up to 10 in. wider! Sometimes the 164-mile journey from De Aar to Beaufort West would take the 25s fourteen hours or more, because this line, which is single track, is booked to carry no less than 56 trains in 24 hours!

What might a busy morning be like at Three Sisters? A double-headed 25 has raced through northwards, followed some 35 minutes later by the arrival of a southbound train which passes into the loop just in time to permit the Cape Town–De Aar passenger train to pass unchecked. The southbound still simmers quietly in the loop, its indolence anticipating another northbound, which soon materialises hard on the passenger train's tail, in the form of yet another double-headed goods. No sooner has the southbound finally got away, before another takes its place in the loop, for now we are anticipating the passage of a Cape Town–Pretoria express which is already within a few miles of Three Sisters. And so it continues.

Three Sisters station takes its name from a trio of strangely shaped koppies situated nearby. These constitute an important Karroo landmark and a well known attraction. Local legend goes that once they were three ill-behaved girls who, as punishment, were turned into stone by witchcraft. It was near here that we made friends with a colony of sixty Rock Dassies who lived in a rocky section of railway embankment. These intensely curious mammals, who are principally indigenous to Africa, were fascinated by our activities and paid us much heed during filming. After a time we were able to recognise eight of them individually, so delightfully varied were their looks and personalities; the short gaps between trains being more than filled by their many antics. As one may imagine our final departure from the desert was characterised by a sadness of unprecedented proportion.

Months later, after our return home, we were bearing the ravages of an English winter when I perchanced to mention to my friend that

132

it was then springtime in South Africa and that the Karroo would be carpeted with a myriad of wild flowers and teeming with beauty. But, I continued, this would be the condensers' last springtime on that line, for already many had been withdrawn. I watched sadness spring to her eyes, for a guiding star from steam's ever darkening constellations seemed to have exploded and was extinguished forever.

S.A.R. No.	Builder	Date
3451	Henschel	1953
3452–3540	North British	1953–4

Leading Dimensions

Cylinders	24 in. × 28 in.
Boiler pressure	225 lb per sq. in.
Driving wheel diameter	5 ft 0 in.
Grate area	70 sq. ft
Tractive effort 85% b.p.	51,410 lb
Total weight f.w.o.	234 tons
Total length	107½ ft
Coal capacity	19 tons
Water capacity	4,400 gallons (make up)
	600 gallons (condensate)

S.A.R. Class 24 2–8–4 'Berkshires' Plate No. 14

The Kaaiman's River Viaduct looked awesome in the gathering gloom of evening. From the hillside I looked down into the sunless hollow which formed the estuary and watched the heavy grey clouds scudding across the ocean, their lack of colour tempered but little by the fluffy whiteness of curling breakers which flicked their way shorewards. The silence only served to enhance the foreboding aura which pervaded the scene. Here indeed was no place to tempt photographic expertise: not that many trains were about, but if there had been, it would have taken a long smoky cavalcade to have tarnished the vista so completely. Leaving the soaring gulls to wail my sentiments, I forlornly returned to the nearby town of George in the hope of a miraculous transformation on the morrow.

Having recently left the Karroo wastes, with their vibrant radiance of sunny colour, the Cape Coastal Belt was a disappointment, for the rich green vegetation which abounded everywhere had been deadened by the mean grey skies. By the time I reached George a drizzle had set in, forcing me to seek good accommodation for that night, so unprepared was I for these cold, humid tantrums. My mood, like the weather, prevailed throughout the evening, so, confining myself indoors, I undertook to read the hotel's literature on the exquisite Cape Province and its famous Garden Route. Beautiful though it was, I could find little sympathy with one line which ran, 'Unlike much of the Republic, the Cape Province enjoys a winter rainfall.' The verb mocked me – for seldom, in this context, would it ever grace a colour photographer's vocabulary!

Fortunately, the following morning dawned bright and it found me back at the viaduct in a refreshed state of mind. It had long been my ambition to picture the rather romantic notion of a 'viaduct over the sea' and though this area is better known for the powerful scenes of GEA Garratts climbing the Montagu Pass, I could not escape the lure of the ocean. The picture shows an S.A.R. 24 Class 2–8–4 heading for Knysna against the watery expanse of the Indian Ocean – what a satisfying relationship the steam locomotive makes with the sea! Kaaiman's River Bridge is situated on the lightly laid line from George to Knysna. This 42-mile-long route, which is worked exclusively by 24 Class engines, is often said to be South Africa's most scenic line, for it gently meanders eastwards along the coast, past ocean, lake, mountain, woodland and meadow, with all the remote splendour of a truly rural branch. A visit to this line provides a refreshing and tranquil interlude amid the heavy 'fortissimo' of South African railways in general.

The 24 Class are the S.A.R.'s only 2–8–4s, being introduced in 1948 as lightly axleloaded engines specifically to replace the multitude

134

of ever-ageing 6th, 7th and 8th Classes. They were given superheaters, along with Walschaerts valve gear and piston valves. One of their principal haunts was the South West Africa section, but they have also abounded throughout much of the Republic, especially on lines possessing only 45 lb track. A particularly distinctive design feature was the provision of steel frames cast integrally with the cylinders and the success of this created a precedent for the same characteristic on the 140 4–8–4s of Class 25. In common with those of the 25s', these frames came from General Steel Castings Co., USA.

Another American feature is their 'Vanderbilt' tender for long range operation in dry areas. These possess cylindrical tanks and are mounted on two six-wheel bogies; although somewhat austere, these American-built tenders are especially attractive to the eye. Exactly 100 24s came from North British between 1949 and 1950, and one of them, No. 3675, perchanced to be the 2,000th locomotive built by that Company. This led to a special ceremony being held at Cape Town when the engine was landed, whereupon she was officially named *Bartholomew Dias* – after the explorer who discovered the Cape. Today, the 24s are still much in evidence, but all have now graduated to the Republic – the South West African section having long since been dieselised.

S.A.R. No.	Builder	Date
3601–3700	North British	1949–50

Leading Dimensions

Cylinders	19 in. × 26 in.
Boiler pressure	200 lb per sq. in.
Driving wheel diameter	4 ft 3 in.
Grate area	36 sq. ft
Tractive effort 85% b.p.	31,290 lb
Total weight f.w.o.	129 tons
Total length	74 ft 9 in.
Coal capacity	9 tons
Water capacity	4,500 gallons

Ex S.A.R. Class 6 4–6–0   Plate No. 27

The Class 6 emerged through the darkness with deep, heavy sighs. Periodically these would accelerate into a tremulous roar as she slipped under the heavy load and with dazed driving wheels the engine would shudder from side to side emitting palls of cinders skywards. Little crackles of fire sprang to life in the darkened veld, depriving the already torrid landscape of whatever sustenance they could. One of the coal-stage men ran promptly to these scintillating outbursts, stamping them out one by one. The action was not new to him, 'We get this game every time she has more than ten on up this bank,' he complained in English tones, 'She wasn't made for it, too big on the wheel – we got her cheap off the main line!' His further remonstrances were lost as he moved out of earshot to quell a more potentially dangerous outburst of fire some distance away. The engine approached languidly and having gained a slightly better control, her wheels still slithered intermittently and further tantrumatic outbursts were promised before the train finally arrived at the coaling stage of Swartkops Power Station. Here was an engine not hesitant to demonstrate her unsuitability for trundling coal waggons around a power station. But suitable or not, the idiosyncrasies of old age have to be reconciled; after all she was nearly eighty years old – was it not her prerogative to slip violently under adverse conditions? She began life in 1897 having come from Neilsons of Glasgow as a Cape Government Railway 6B Class.

Swartkops, a suburb of Port Elizabeth, is a fascinating combination of tidal waste land, salt pans, industry and modern development; the combination of these providing a unique atmosphere. The story goes that it was named after a carbon factory which threw black smuts over the marshy, coastal area upon which the township is now situated. Land reclamation has largely taken place since 1952 and today it is difficult to believe that this bustling town had a population of less than 500 people twenty-five years ago; it is an intermediate station on the Port Elizabeth–Uitenhage service. The entire area is dominated by the Swartkops Power Station, an enthralling rectangular structure with six tall, slender chimneys. It was built in the 1950s, and a characteristic feature is its lack of cooling towers owing to the close proximity of both the tidal Swartkops River and the sea. Apart from solemnly presiding over the town, the structure can be seen many miles away and it serves as an excellent landmark, so unmistakable is the remarkable form. The Port Elizabeth municipality now owns the Power Station, having taken it over from E.S.C.O.M. in 1956.

Swartkops Power Station obtained this 6B from the S.A.R. Sydenham depot in 1972 at a price of 1,200 Rand, but it cost several times this figure to put her into proper working order. Prior to the 6B's arrival, traffic was operated by a charming R.S.H. 0–4–0ST, No. 7685 of 1953. This engine, which is of a very standard shape, despite the 3 ft 6 in. gauge, is painted blue and named *Swartkops* and from a distance she looks identical to many of Britain's latter-day industrial 0–4–0STs. Other Class 6 engines still lie abandoned at Sydenham, having once been engaged on the Uitenhage runs. Locomotive operations are limited at Swartkops; the engines being restricted to moving coal from adjacent S.A.R. sidings up to the station boilers and storage dumps – a distance of little over half a mile.

The Class 6 engines form one of the most important types in South African locomotive history, with no less than 268 basically similar engines being built. They were destined to operate throughout the Republic with the exception of Natal. The class was designed at Salt River Works, Cape Town, under H. M. Beatty, Locomotive Superintendent of the Cape Government Railway, as an express passenger version of his celebrated Class 7 4–8–0s of 1892. The first appeared in 1893 and though principally intended for the C.G.R. some were also built for the Orange Free State Railway (O.V.G.S.), whilst others were passed to the Imperial Military Railway (I.M.R.) during the Boer War; all of these passed into Central South African Railway (C.S.A.R.) stock after 1902, when the war ended. After formation of the S.A.R. in 1910, the 6s became standard main line power until their eventual displacement from top duties led to their becoming maids-of-all-work as an important mixed traffic class. As the year progressed and power demands continually increased, the ubiquitous 6s, though still on the scene, suffered further demotions to branch lines, pilot and trip work and eventually shunting. Such scattered remnants as now exist are all sold to industry, principally collieries, and despite their widely varied capabilities they are somewhat stifled on heavy coal hauls – as the 6B clearly demonstrates. During World War II sixteen were sold to the Sudan Government Railway, whilst others have gone to the Benguela Railway, Angola.

Listed below is a summary of their building sequence. Most had plate frames, but all were unsuperheated with slide valves and Stephenson Link Motion, except the final two in 1904. The 6F/6G variants were slightly larger in cylinder diameter and boiler pressure by $\frac{1}{2}$ in. and 20 lb per sq. in. respectively. Originally all had round-topped boilers but many were later rebuilt with Belpairs until, under Watson's régime, a new round-topped boiler was provided. This was even fitted to some of the Belpair conversions; the engine illustrated has a round-top boiler.

Swartkops Power Station has since acquired a diesel locomotive, so placing the Class 6 in jeopardy, and it now seems that little future exists for this ailing remnant of one of the most important classes of express passenger engine ever to run in Africa.

Class	No. Built	Builder	Date	
6	40	Dubs	1893	
6A	17	Dubs/Sharp Stewart	1896	
6A	33	Dubs	1897	
6B	23	Dubs/Neilson	1897	
6B	15	Neilson	1898	
6B	16	Neilson Reid	1898	
6C	28	Sharp Stewart/Dubs/ Neilson Reid	1896/7	O.V.G.S.
6D	33	Neilson Reid	1898	Greater heating surface
6E	6	Sharp Stewart	1898	O.V.G.S.
6F	2	Sharp Stewart	1900	Bar frames
6G	8	Alco	1901	Bar frames
6H	21	Neilson Reid	1901	
6J	14	Neilson Reid	1902	Bar frames
6K	10	Baldwin	1901	Bar frames
6L	2	North British	1904	Superheaters and piston valves

Leading Dimensions 6B

Cylinders	17 in. × 26 in.
Boiler pressure	180 lb per sq. in.
Driving wheel diameter	4 ft 6 in.
Grate area	17 sq. ft
Tractive effort 85% b.p.	21,290 lb
Total weight f.w.o.	80 tons approx.
Total length	54 ft approx.
Coal capacity	8 tons (XE Tender)
Water capacity	2,850 gallons (XE Tender)

SOUTH AFRICA: Eastern Province Cement Co. 'Baldwin Pacific'

A chance comment made by a stranger at Swartkops led us to discover this remarkable Baldwin 'Pacific'. We were in Port Elizabeth to see 'Pacifics', but we did not expect to find a little red one which looked as if it had tumbled from the pages of a Reverend Audrey book, for our preoccupations were centred upon the S.A.R. 16CR 4–6–2s which, with their peculiar dashing elegance, were enacting the Uitenhage suburban services. If the Reverend Audrey ever sets eye upon this engine, it may well appear in one of his future books, albeit in a thinly disguised form! Not that our informant described the engine as a Baldwin 'Pacific', he simply instructed us to go up to the huge Cement Works in Port Elizabeth where he guaranteed we would find, 'A nifty little thing on narrow gauge tracks.' We ventured towards the afore-said venue with a mixture of faith, hope and trepidation – for such a rare prize had been promised.

Faith, hope and trepidation; how inherent these feelings are when undertaking researches in other countries, for they occur time and time again. In this case our faith was borne of a basic respect for our informant; after all, even the most diligent researches can seldom ignore such chance information. Our hope sprang from an intent to retain an open mind, nevertheless uninformed and emotive tales from laymen are a constant hazard to the specialised researcher, and we, through bitter experience, well knew what fruitless deviations these could cause. But any such hope bears trepidation, for 'unexpected jewels' can sometimes startle even the most scientifically conducted probings, whilst to anyone of a slightly romantic disposition the likelihood of unexpected finds is so much greater – so easily are such people coerced by the charms of the obvious!

Possessing these sentiments, we eventually arrived at the head office of the Eastern Province Cement Co. Ltd, and with a meekness not unlike that of two scruffy urchins approaching a potentially irate neighbour for the retrieval of a ball which had been carelessly kicked onto his property, said, 'Have you got a steam engine here?' 'Why? Want to buy it?' retorted the large, uniformed commissionaire. 'We'll pay them to take it away!' called a man from the next office who, upon presenting himself before us, asked the nature of our business. I recounted the story our casual acquaintance had told, adding the request that if such a gem existed we might be permitted to see it. And so we were chaperoned through a maze of dusty, white-coated buildings until, upon reaching some sidings, we beheld rows of little 2 ft 0 in. gauge waggons loaded with cement. 'Where is No. 2?' our guide shouted to some nearby workmen. The reply was lost to me for it came in the Afrikaans tongue, but the gist of it was that we must wait some hours for the engine to return, as she was out collecting a load of cement from the 2 ft 0 in. gauge connection with the S.A.R. at Chelsea, some 12 miles distant. We waited at the engine shed for our prize to manifest itself and were afforded a magnificent, panoramic view of Port Elizabeth – already becoming spangled with the first lights of early dusk.

As is generally known, the S.A.R. have considerable 2 ft 0 in. gauge track, both in Cape Province and Natal. The former system's main line runs from Port Elizabeth to Avontuur and this handles traffic from the extensive limestone quarries at Lourie. The S.A.R. bring the stone to Chelsea, whereupon it is forwarded to the Works by the Cement Co.'s private line. We were most fortunate to find the Baldwin working for normally operations are handled by a Hunslet diesel and the general feeling was that No. 2 would not survive much longer; the arrival of a second diesel being imminent!

She was built in 1930 as Baldwin No. 61269: a locomotive capable of operating on 35 lb rail and able to negotiate 165 ft radius curves. The original Baldwin boiler has unfortunately been replaced by a Hunslet one which lacks the characteristic sandboxes placed either side of the dome – these having been relegated to rectangular boxes on the engine's running plate. However, mitigation for this loss is provided by her fabulous spark arresting chimney – a feature absent from the original boiler! The engine possesses such refinements as Baldwin steam brakes on both driving and tender axles in addition to the normal hand screw brake on the tender. Other enhancements are Stone Electric Generators which light up large 14 in. diameter headlamps, one on the smokebox, the other on the tender back. Also she has one of the nicest chime whistles I have ever heard; its melodiousness might almost be described as fragrant!

When originally delivered, this now unique engine was blessed with an olive green livery and aluminium lining. Her tender was boldly inscribed 'EASTERN PROVINCE CEMENT CO. LTD' whilst a large 'No. 2' appeared on the front numberplate, cab panels and tender rear. Although ending her days in the improved red livery, as shown, she was, by this time, devoid of lining, lettering and number. Nevertheless, this charming little Baldwin provided a delightful extra to latterday steam operations around Port Elizabeth and looked extremely quaint as she chugged her trainload of limestone up to the factory with the 'friendly city' spreading across the landscape to the rear.

Leading Dimensions

Cylinders	13½ in. × 18 in.
Boiler pressure	160 lb per sq. in.
Driving wheel diameter	3 ft 0 in.
Grate area	14·2 sq. ft
Axle loading	6¾ tons approx.
Total heating surface	783 sq. ft
Tractive effort 85% b.p.	12,350 lb
Total weight f.w.o.	50½ tons approx.
Coal capacity	4½ tons
Water capacity	1,700 gallons

S.A.R. 16R/16CR 'Pacifics' Plates Nos. 17, 23, 24

One of the most characteristic aspects of an all-steam railway was the densely operated suburban services which graced the world's major cities. Almost inevitably special locomotives were designed for this work, but the worldwide demise of steam traction has already passed most of these into history. Understandably, because the steam locomotive is relatively unsuited to the heavy demands imposed by such services. Heavy trains need to be worked up to high speeds between frequent stops. There is a demand for a quick turnaround at either end of the line, and also for clean air in densely populated suburbs. None of these show steam power in its most favourable light. Obviously the model for such operations is electric traction especially when this can be energised from the ever-increasing main line electrifications out of large cities. It is little wonder that suburban trains operated entirely by steam have largely become a thing of the past, but one notable exception is the remarkable services over all, or various parts, of the 21-mile line from Port Elizabeth to Uitenhage. These sprightly services are now world famous because they sport 56 trains per weekday, all 100% steam operated – principally by 'Pacifics' of World War I vintage.

The stars in this drama are the 16CR Class and the stirring activity generated by them with these trains is of a truly exceptional nature. Unceasingly they race through the suburbs of this modern city,

Swartkops Power Station

animating the environs with an intense puthering 'whoosh', followed
by the wooden hum of clicking coaches. Some trains load up to
11 vehicles, representing a 350-ton gross weight, but nevertheless
high speeds are invariably reached. Indeed, certain trains are
scheduled to cover the 21 miles in 47 minutes, with eight intermediate
stops and many adverse gradients. A keen spirit exists amongst the
Sydenham enginemen involved on these runs and many 'Pacifics' are
maintained in a dazzling condition and are enlivened by numerous
embellishments; note for example the engine's nameplate and ornamental smoke deflectors on plate 24, not to mention the array of
adornments gracing the smokebox! Many 16CR numberplates are a
picture within themselves, often having sensitively chosen colours,
which apart from contrasting with each other, greatly enhance the
plate's brass lettering and rims. Some cab interiors might be likened
to a spotless nineteenth-century kitchen with a gleaming stove, varied
culinary utensils, voluminous shining copper work and polished
floorboards and walls.

From such a fabric must emerge some legendary-like figures who,
with their own engines, are dedicated to a partial transposition of
punctuality, cleanliness and speed into accretions of their own ego –
and why not? After all, life is for living these men will tell you!
Unofficial speeds of up to 70 m.p.h. are allegedly reached between
stations only 2½ miles apart, but such speeds being well over the
S.A.R.'s permitted maximum, cannot be enumerated here! But

142

The 100% steam-operated suburban service from Port Elizabeth: principally 16R/16CR 'Pacifics' of World War I vintage

AS FROM 2.7.73 PORT ELIZABETH-UITENHAGE MONDAYS–FRIDAYS

Stations	210	208	232	220	226	218	216	224	228	236	248	255	266
Port Elizabeth dep:	5.20	5.35	6.06	6.15	6.34	6.56	7.06	8.32	9.45	11.30	13.10	14.20	16.10
North End	5.23	5.38	6.09	6.18	6.37	6.59	7.09	8.35	9.48	11.33	13.13	14.23	16.13
Sydenham	5.28	5.43	6.14	6.23	6.42	7.04	7.14	8.40	9.53	11.38	13.18	14.28	16.18
New Brighton	5.33	5.48	6.19	6.28	6.47	7.10	7.19	8.44	9.58	11.43	13.23	14.33	16.23
Swartkops Junction	5.39	5.54	6.25	6.34			7.24	8.49		11.49	13.28	14.39	16.29
Redhouse		6.01		6.43			7.30	8.55		11.55	13.34	14.46	16.35
Perseverance		6.07		6.49			7.36	9.01		12.00	13.40	14.52	16.41
Despatch		6.14		7.01			7.43	9.12		12.07	13.46	14.59	16.48
De Mist		6.24		7.14			7.54	9.20		12.14	13.54	15.06	17.04
Uitenhage arr:		6.29		7.19			7.58	9.25		12.19	13.59	15.11	17.09

Stations	270	272	278	276	244	246	284	260	288	294	308	296	298
Port Elizabeth dep:	16.37	16.42	17.00	17.10	17.32	17.43	17.53	18.05	18.15	19.30	20.30	22.10	23.05
North End	16.40	16.45	17.03	17.13	17.35	17.46	17.56	18.08	18.18	19.33	20.36	22.13	23.08
Sydenham	16.45	16.50	17.08	17.18	17.40	17.51	18.01	18.13	18.23	19.38	20.43	22.18	23.13
New Brighton	16.50	16.55	17.13	17.23	17.45	17.57	18.06	18.17	18.27	19.43	20.48	22.23	23.18
Swartkops Junction		17.01	17.19	17.29			18.11	18.23	18.32	19.48	20.55	22.28	23.23
Redhouse		17.07		17.35			18.17		18.38	19.55	21.04	22.34	23.29
Perseverance		17.16		17.41			18.23		18.43	20.01	21.13	22.39	23.34
Despatch		17.23		17.47			18.30		18.50	20.07	21.21	22.46	23.41
De Mist		17.30		17.55			18.39		18.57	20.15	21.30	22.52	23.48
Uitenhage arr:		17.35		18.01			18.44		19.02	20.20	21.35	22.58	23.53

Each outward working corresponds with a return trip home. Reduced services operate over weekends.

certainly these trains constitute South Africa's fastest steam operations with punctuality guaranteed almost to the second. The enthusiasm which emanates from Sydenham shed is a tonic for a spirit tarnished by the dour unimaginativeness shown by so many motive power administrations and it needs to go on record as one of the true high-spots of the current S.A.R. scene. These are now the last important workings for the 'Pacific' locomotive in the entire South African Republic.

On plate 17, I have tried to capture the essentiality of these vivid operations as a 16CR, all out for Uitenhage, takes its vengeance on the sunny skies. Plate 24, whilst still emphasising rapidity, takes a more introspective view: the train being faithfully duplicated in the tranquil water beneath the embankment. Notice how the 'Pacific' has hit the straight with a totally combusted fire, only swirling up exhaust steam into the atmosphere. Then, with an ominous stealth, the scene darkens, as a few shovelfulls of coal are applied, so splitting the exhaust trail into a perfect separation of steam and smoke, again perfectly duplicated by the waters beneath.

These 'Pacifics' are fine-looking engines and are well set in the Hendrie tradition. During their years of eminence they worked all main line passenger traffic in the Transvaal and further undertook express duties in both the Orange Free State and Natal. As a class they were similar to Hendrie's 15s, page 145, which were introduced simultaneously – many parts being interchangeable. Originally built with Belpair boilers, the class was later fitted with round-top ones under Watson's régime in the 1930s when they received his standard 2B boiler. The table below gives the order and date of building. Basically all batches were alike, but the 16Cs had combustion chambers – as did the 15As of the same period; this later variant improved an already superlative engine. Watson's reboilering gave them the revised classifications of 16R instead of 16 for the 1914 batch and 16CR for both the 16B/Cs; but nowadays all are regarded as one class.

Over more recent years the demand for heavier expresses combined with more modern forms of motive power have swept these elegant machines off the main lines and today many are sadly demoted to shunting and trip work. However, the Port Elizabeth–Uitenhage suburban services still provide the 16CRs with an opportunity to testify their former brilliance and, furthermore, it has given them a belated fame, for sixty years after their inception, the class's twilight receives a crown of distinction.

144

Original Class	S.A.R. Nos.	Builder	Date
16 (16R)	790–801	North British	1914
16B (16CR)	802–811	North British	1917
16C (16CR)	812–821	North British	1919
16C (16CR)	822–841	North British	1921

Leading Dimensions 16R*/16CR 'Pacifics'

Cylinders	22 in. × 26 in.	
Boiler pressure	200 lb per sq. in.	(16R: 190 lb)
Driving wheel diameter	5 ft 3 in.	(16R: 5 ft 0 in.)
Grate area	37 sq. ft	
Tractive effort 85% b.p.	33,890 lb	
Total weight f.w.o.	149 tons approx.	
Total length	67 ft approx.	
Coal capacity	12 tons (M.T. Tender)	
Water capacity	6,000 gallons (M.T. Tender)	

*Under Watson, classes 16B/C had their driving wheel diameters and boiler pressure slightly increased.

S.A.R. 15AR Class 4–8–2   Plates Nos. 13, 16, 37

In 1913 a need arose for heavier power to handle mixed traffic across the Orange Free State and under Chief Mechanical Engineer Hendrie an enlarged 4–8–2 was designed, being a graduation from the earlier 12 and 14 classes. The new type was designated Class 15, the first ten coming from the North British Works in 1914 and these were promptly sent to Bloemfontein depot. In D. F. Holland's marvellous *Steam Locomotives of the South African Railways* he quotes a delightful, if unconfirmed, tale of one Bloemfontein driver who, upon arriving for duty, saw the first 15 Class in the depot yard and 'promptly went home to bed, believing himself to be suffering from hallucinations'! Certainly they were the largest conventional engine up to that time; a fact augmented by their slender businesslike appearance. After the first ten engines, all later examples were fitted with a combustion chamber to reduce their boiler tube lengths and these variants were known as 15As. In fact the 15A also appeared in 1914 and by 1925 no less than 129 examples had been put into traffic, having come from the works of North British, Beyer Peacock and Maffei; this total includes the ten original 15 Class. Over many years these stalwarts operated successfully between Kimberley and Cape Town and were able to run up very high mileages between overhauls.

So the engines ran until the coming to office of A. G. Watson, C.M.E. of South Africa Railways from 1929 to 1936, whereupon he determined to introduce an extensive programme of standard boilers and parts in a cost-cutting rationalisation programme. Under this scheme, he dismissed the Belpair firebox in favour of the round-top type and dispensed with combustion chambers. Accordingly, the 15As were fitted with his standard 2A boiler taking the classification of 15AR. Very few survived this reboilering although I did see a 15A at Witbank in 1973 and a lovely engine she looked, for Watson's standard boilers did little to aid visual differentiation between classes and many older types lost their former distinctiveness. One notable feature of Watson's reboilerings was the emergence of the rearward sloping cut-away cabs. He did this in order to render all firebox stays accessible without removing the cab.

However, these 15ARs are a pleasant engine to behold and a great number still survive, although nowadays the class is widely distributed, as more modern forms of power have displaced them from main line work. In addition to the engines elucidated above, a further thirty came from the works of Montreal and Alco between 1918 and 1921 – presumably because British works were unable to guarantee prompt delivery so soon after World War I. These were simply a Transatlantic version, having such American features as bar-frames and high running plates. Naturally these too succumbed to Watson's No. 2 boiler, although they retained their high footplating. Now classified 15BR, these transatlantics are, to all intents and purposes, identical with the others.

One marring aspect of the 15AR, and one which afflicts almost all other South African steamers too, is the saddening way in which the ugly outside feed pipes lead up to an uncased clack valve placed immediately before the dome. One yearns for the handsomely encased dome and top feed combination of many engines indigenous to Britain, along with their attendant feed pipes neatly hugging the boiler's contours. The clumsy ineptness of this South African feature seems quite out of character with the distinctive lineage of their engines!

Late one evening, I recall watching a 15AR at Sydenham shed, Port Elizabeth. Several were present, but one in particular, No. 2083, the subject of plate 37, stood separate from the rest in that she was animated and tense and surrounded by that pregnant air so peculiar to steam locomotives. Of course she was waiting to go out and I was drawn to the side of her silhouetted form as a night moth might be drawn to a blaze of phosphorescence. The engine was bursting with energy and as I drew alongside the injector went on with a musical singing roar, indicating the impeccable order in which Sydenham maintains its engines. Simultaneously, the fireman began to hose down the coals and footplate, the vapour muting the dancing orange reflections of the fire and throwing the entire engine into a haloed incandescent aura. The injector and spraying water, combined with the fire and now whistling safety valves, all contributed to a symphony which seemed to evoke the very soul of steam. Suddenly with a violent 'whoosh' the injector spat out and a few rounds of coal onto the fire raised a heavy umber smoke into a sky already flushed with sodium light. The sanders were tested before a splash of steam off the cylinder cocks precipitated 2083's departure and slowly the 15AR moved off into the night, the driving wheels spinning with a resounding series of clanks accompanied by an urgency of steam fluttering around her chimney top. Then, as if she had not been expressive enough, the engine blew down, issuing a tumultuous pall of steam across the shed yard; initially turning the adjacent engines into ghostly forms before blotting them out completely and turning the darkness into rippling white clouds which danced and effervesced. Eventually a dimly-lit tender lamp became our only evidence of 2083, until that in turn, became swallowed by darkness. Her whistle now haunted a distant suburb.

Later that night, I thought of 2083 forging the 400-ton train over the arduous route to Klipplaat, as we, from the comfort of our beds, may well give mind to the engine crews and their mounts enacting steam's last fling in the Cape Peninsula. Yet I wanted to be there, both on the footplate and, in an all seeing way, at the lineside to watch 2083 flogging over the 1 in 70 grades with a flickering blaze of russet dancing in the exhaust trail and a chattering wake of merchandise bowling along behind. I willed to hear the heavy clanging shovel ringing on the tender backplate, to listen to the syncopated plashes of steam rhythmically flirting around the cylinder drains and to watch her vibrant silhouette rolling past remote trees and rocks as acrid in form as the engine itself.

But long before 2083 reached Klipplaat that night, my dimensional journey had crumbled and, incapable of further emotion, I fell into a felicitous slumber.

147

15, 15A, 15B Classes – Virtually all now 15AR/15BR Classes

No. Series	Original Class	Builder	Date
1561–1570	15	North British	1914
1571–1575	15A	North British	1914
1781–1828	15A	North British	1914–20
1839–1858	15A	Beyer Peacock	1920
1961–1970	15A	Beyer Peacock	1925
2011–2025	15A	North British	1921
2080–2100	15A	Maffei	1921

Transatlantic Version

1829–1838	15B	Montreal	1918
1971–1990	15B	Alco	1921

Leading Dimensions 15AR Class

Cylinders	22 in. × 28 in.
Boiler pressure	190 lb per sq. in.
Driving wheel diameter	4 ft 9 in.
Grate area	37 sq. ft
Tractive effort 85% b.p.	38,400 lb
Total length	71 ft 6½ in. approx.
Total weight f.w.o.	155 tons approx.

S.A.R. GMA/GMAM Class 4–8–2 + 2–8–4 Garratt
Plates Nos. 30, 31, 32

Apart from being one of the first to acquire the Garratt locomotive, South Africa's railways have since become the world's largest user of these engines. Garratts first went to South Africa in 1920 and quickly proved themselves superior to the Mallet type, which was widely in use at that time. The nature of South Africa's railways is dictated by the immense inland plateau nearly a mile higher than sea level, accordingly steep gradients have to be surmounted by inland routes from the coast. This, combined with a difficult terrain in general, frequently meant a railway abounding in heavy gradients, 'S' curves and horse-shoe bends, and furthermore, set onto relatively lightly laid track. After all, it was not financially possible to construct the railways of this new country to anything approaching standards common in the wealthier and longer established lands. But, paradoxically, South Africa's rich industrial potential soon demanded that huge tonnages be

148

carried by her railways, frequently over long distances in difficult terrain. So arose the perennial question of increasingly heavy traffic which was an essential part of the country's economic framework, needing to be carried over lightly built lines. It is small wonder then that the Garratt locomotive has held considerable sway since its inception, as it is eminently suitable for working under such conditions. Let us consider its principal advantages: on a Garratt engine the boiler and firebox are free of axles and so can be built to whatever size is needed, both for ample generation of steam and proper combustion of gases by the provision of a deep firebox. Conversely, as the wheels are free of the boiler they can be made to whatever diameter is considered best. By placing the engine's wheels and cylinders under a front water unit and rear coal unit, situated either side of the boiler, the engine's weight is spread over a wide area. Then, simply by articulating these two units from the boiler, a large powerful locomotive can be built, which is capable of moving heavy loads over curved, graded and lightly laid lines. Altogether, the S.A.R. has had over 400 Garratt locomotives, many British-built, and the majority remain in service to this day – the last ones being completed as recently as 1968!

These GMAs are an excellent example in illustrating the application of the Garratt locomotive to operating necessities, for they are direct descendants of the GM Garratt introduced by Beyer Peacock in 1938 specifically to work between Johannesburg and Zeerust on the Mafeking line. This route, which demanded powerful engines for the heavy through workings into Rhodesia, abounded in severe gradients some as steep as 1 in 40, whilst furthermore it was laid with 60 lb rail incapable of taking anything heavier than a 15 ton axle load. Prior to the GMs introduction, the authorities were having to double-head 19D 4–8–2s (page 164) which were obviously uneconomical and the Garratts were designed to be equivalent to a pair of 19Ds. The GMs provided the complete answer and with an axle load less than 15 tons they possessed, at 85% boiler pressure, a 68,800 lb tractive effort compared with 36,100 lb for a 19D. However, in order to fall within this axle loading, the GMs' coal and water carrying capacities had to be reduced to 10 tons and 1,600 gallons only and to augment the water supply a separate auxiliary tank holding 6,750 gallons was attached to the engine. This was the first time such an application had been made to a Garratt engine, but its relative simplicity created a precedent for the 120 very similar engines of classes GMA/GMAM which were put into service between 1952 and 1958 as maximum power branch line engines. Within themselves the GMA/GMAM differed only in coal and water carrying capacities, but they represented an improvement on the GMs in having cast steel, one-piece bed frames and roller bearings on all axles. Furthermore, they have the distinction of being the most numerous Garratt class in the world, whilst they must surely be the world's most powerful steam engines operating over 60 lb rail! GMAs have worked in many parts of South Africa, especially the Mafeking, East London and Lourenco Marques main lines, along with many routes in Natal.

The greatest concentration of GMAs is at Masons Mill depot, Pietermaritzburg, and from here they work the notorious and tortuously difficult lines up to Franklin and Greytown. Pietermaritzburg has become synonymous with Garratts, for it is now celebrated as having the largest Garratt allocation in the world. Upon visiting this depot one witnesses these grotesque and restless engines looming out of the gloom and it is an intensely moving experience. I feel that one of the most awe-inspiring aspects of a steam locomotive is the hint of grotesqueness which many have. This is particularly so with the GMAs with their hideous bunkers and tanks – which frown downwards at a most unnerving angle – and their auxiliary tanks, which are equally potent looking pieces of ironmongery! Strength and power are clearly two more fragments of steam's universal appeal. But is aggression? How many locomotives truly symbolise aggression? I cannot think of a more ferocious engine than the GMA and when standing between them in the depot one gains the chilling sensation that they will suddenly seize upon you and swallow you up. The chuntering, rumbling and pulsating sounds which epitomise these deeply intense machines is like a cacophony inside the belly of some enormous prehistoric creature; the whole locomotive being a mass of seething energy.

Out on the road their potency continues undiminished, especially when running in pairs – imagine two in tandem, flat out, attacking a 1 in 30 grade on the Natal escarpment; the two engines separated by auxiliary tanks and eight cylinders issuing a pounding roar. Not that the loads they carry are heavy in relative terms, for between Greytown and Schroeders two GMAs take only 850 tons, whilst one handles 360 tons, but these gradients are remarkably severe, even for secondary lines and the locomotive effort needs to be far more than doubled when lifting a train over a 1 in 30 bank compared with a 1 in 60. Such a cavalcade is possibly as great a motive power spectacle as any in the world today. Playfully and powerfully they will amble when under easy steam, like tigers romping in fun, but when a gradient turns against them their character is transformed, and they become anguished beasts deprived of their sanity.

The pictures show GMAs in action on the sugar and lumber line up to Greytown and plate 30 depicts one of these mechanically-stoked giants hitting the base of a 1 in 37 bank. She was built in 1958 by Beyer Peacock of Manchester. The activity and tension can be sensed as the engine, with heavy fire and singing safety valves, pugnaciously bites into the gradient, for it is 'all hell' to get that tonnage over the top. What a relationship this thrusting colossus makes with the verdant stillness of the conifer plantation; the umbrella of black smoke vitally cohesing the two together. Plate 31 is a detail study of this action and I think sights such as this rival the great days of American steam, generally acknowledged to be the greatest spectacle of all, in this now quickly vanishing era of man's history.

S.A.R. Nos.	Builder	Date
4051–75	Henschel	1952
4076–98	Beyer Peacock	1956
4099–4110	North British	1956
4111–4120	North British	1958
4121–4130	Beyer Peacock	1958
4131–4140	North British	1958
4141–4170	Henschel	1954

GMA/GMAM Leading Dimensions

Cylinders (4)	$20\frac{1}{2}$ in. × 26 in.
Boiler pressure	200 lb per sq. in.
Driving wheel diameter	4 ft 6 in.
Grate area	63·2 sq. ft
Tractive effort 85% b.p.	68,800 lb
Total weight f.w.o.	187 tons
Total length	94 ft (without auxiliary tank)
Coal capacity	$11\frac{1}{2}$ tons (GMAM 14 tons)
Water capacity	1,650 gallons + auxiliary tank 6,810 gallons (GMAM 2,100 gallons)

R.R. 14A 2-6-2 + 2-6-2 Garratt   Plates Nos. 2, 19, 25

'First you must see the West Nicholson branch because there you will find 14A and 16A Garratts and you will also be able to see the train with a double-headed Garratt which works between here and Balla Balla – this is one of the few double-headed Garratt turns in the world! So you must spend at least a day on this section before you go onto the Wankie line.' The speaker was Chris Butcher of the Rhodesian Railways – a noted authority on Rhodesian engines, and the scene was the reception at a Bulawayo hotel. I had just arrived in the country. 'Let's take an afternoon spin out towards Balla Balla in my car,' volunteered Chris, 'We're bound to pick up at least one 14A somewhere en route!' I needed little persuasion and after a brief lunch we were soon speeding along a modern highway heading for the bush and the remoteness of Balla Balla.

'It's strange to think,' Chris shouted over the engine's roar, 'what an exception to the rule double-headed Garratt operations are. After all, the Garratt was basically introduced to avoid the double-heading of orthodox "straight" locomotives. But this line is an exception and it cannot be avoided. Let me explain the circumstances,' he continued. 'The heavy gradients on this route lie between here and Balla Balla, from there on to West Nicholson the line evens out somewhat. Now, for example, a 16A can bring up to 955 tons from West Nicholson, but she must reduce this load to 685 tons at Balla Balla before proceeding on to Bulawayo owing to heavy 1 in 50 gradients. This leaves a surplus of loads at Balla Balla and in order to clear these, train 303 leaves Bulawayo in the early hours of the morning headed by two Garratts, either two 14As, two 16As, or one of each, depending on the availability of engines and the load to be brought in. Obviously nothing larger than a 16A can use the branch because weight restrictions forbid it and even now the two engines have to be separated by a waggon to spread out their weight. The 14As have an axle loading of 13¾ tons and the 16As are just over 14½ tons. When they reach Balla, the two Garratts turn on a specially made triangle and, after a brief stop for water and fire tending, they collect the surplus loads and set off about mid-morning for Bulawayo. If it should be two 16As they can bring in 1,380 tons. As you will see, this is quite a busy line, it carries a lot of limestone for Bulawayo Cement Works, and also handles a lot of cattle trains.'

We were now in wild country and across the rugged terrain on our left I noticed a pall of smoke rising up from where I assumed the

152

line to be. Eagerly I cried out, 'There's something over there.' 'No, forget it,' replied Chris, 'That's just a veld blaze, the railway lies miles behind that and we don't see it for some distance yet!'

Chris had traversed this route many times and he told me that this strange and aloof branch was his favourite stretch of railway. This surprised me at the time, but upon becoming familiar with the line I understood exactly what he meant. Its remoteness had a great appeal, for the line passed entirely through hilly, rocky country covered in stunted bush. Its twists, curves, gradients, bridges, isolated watering points and intermittent lonely wayside crossings all culminated in its special appeal and provided the line with an indefinably unique atmosphere. Furthermore, Chris told me that the route was almost one hundred per cent operated by these marvellous Garratts, though occasionally a Class 12 4–8–2 might put in an appearance in times of motive power shortages. Chris narrated tales of innumerable Saturdays spent on this seventy-year-old railway and brought with him a large bundle of pictures taken over a number of years.

Our arrival at Balla Balla did in fact produce a 14A, busily assembling its waggons prior to continuing on to Bulawayo. Plate 25 shows one of these engines taking refreshment here whilst heading a goods from West Nicholson. What a sight she makes having been freshly outshopped from Bulawayo Works – an ex-works Garratt in 1973! Notice the cataract of water splashing over the motion and wheels; see how it engenders a vivid blaze of impressionism. The Garratt boy, whose duty it is to water the engine, is engaged elsewhere and his lack of attention has allowed water to plash vigorously around the engine. Notice also the priceless piece of railwayana provided by the water column beautifully decked in black and yellow stripes, whilst the presence of blow down and smoke completes an evocative study; a study bathed in magnificent African sunlight and set against a hint of tranquil sky.

I was well entertained by Chris during my visit to Bulawayo and on a subsequent day we again made a foray onto the West Nicholson line. This was a day when several specials were running and it promised us a busy time with our cameras. The plate 'Over Crocodile River' was from this session and it shows up the intrinsic aspects of a Garratt locomotive's anatomy. See the 14A's large, fat boiler and deeply set firebox and the way in which the front and rear driving units are articulated from the engine.

153

Crocodile River was totally in the wilds except for the railway. Apart from its more obvious inhabitants, the spot abounded in birds and between trains we were kept well amused by the Grey Lourie with his supercilious cries of 'go away', 'go away', along with an array of less definable yells and utterances. The louries were not too keen on 14As, but they were infinitely less keen on us, and for over an hour they continued to bombard us with a multitude of vociferous insults. The louries, persistent though they were, could be ignored, but what of the crocodiles which lurked amid the reeds and murky water? How could we give good attention to locomotives with such creatures from Erebus in our midst? Some crocodiles are very aggressive and may attack! So the acute tension, felt in making this picture, came partly from the Garratt and partly from a fear of one of these reptiles suddenly emerging from the reeds in front of me! When a mass of cloud drifts across the skies it completely transforms the mood of the landscape and here the 14A's smoke and steam are echoing the fabric of this mottled sky.

The 14As are direct descendants from the 14th Class Garratt of 1928, being simply a modernised version, possessing such improvements as streamlined tanks, power reversers, and Beyer Peacock's self-adjusting pivots. They were built to operate the R.R.'s secondary lines following the increase in traffic after World War II. Their delivery coincided with the 16A Garratts, which in turn were a modernised version of the earlier 16th. Although looking rather different from their predecessors, the 14As were, in fact, almost identical in dimensions and, as such, they stem directly from the original Rhodesian Garratts of 1926, the 13th Class, upon which the 14s were very closely modelled.

Today, steam power is at a low ebb in Rhodesia and though these Garratts are engaged in certain other duties, their principal haunt is now between Bulawayo and West Nicholson. Along with the 16As, they are now expected to share the power monopoly of this busy line until such time as the civil engineer can upgrade the track sufficiently to permit the use of diesels. Upgrading work has already been in operation for some time but many earthworks still need considerable revision before the R.R. can finally dispense with these historic 14As; engines whose family lineage goes back to the introduction of the Rhodesian Garratt itself, fifty years ago.

R.R. No.	Builder	Date
508–525	Beyer Peacock	1953/4

Leading Dimensions

Cylinders (4)	16 in. × 24 in.
Boiler pressure	180 lb per sq. in.
Driving wheel diameter	4 ft 0 in.
Grate area	38·6 sq. ft
Tractive effort 85% b.p.	39,168 lb
Total weight f.w.o.	132 tons
Total length	72½ ft
Coal capacity	7 tons
Water capacity	Front tank: 2,460 gallons
	Rear tank: 1,140 gallons

SOUTH AFRICA: Ex Rhodesian 16th Class 2–8–2 + 2–8–2 Garratt
Plate No. 33

One might arbitrarily assume that a truly vintage steam engine must be a nineteenth-century one, for seventy-five years would seem a respectable period for such an honour. But different criteria might be applied to Garratts, for despite the multiplicity of types built and their widespread distribution, the first ones did not see the light of day until 1911; so possibly any Garratt built prior to 1930 might fairly be regarded as vintage. My surmise is hypothetical; but it does appear to have validity when discussing the Rhodesian Railways 16th Class, for the ancient lineation of these engines is a joy to behold; notice the old style of completely square tanks and bunker, two features which can generally be said to date a Garratt.

The Rhodesian Railways have been big users of the Garratt engine ever since its introduction there in 1926 with the 2–6–2 + 2–6–2 13th/14th classes, but when these 16s appeared in 1929 as the third in accession, they were to undertake much heavier duties and they possessed a capability to lift 700-ton trains over 1 in 40 gradients. The initial eight were put into traffic between 1929 and 1930, having come from Beyer Peacock of Manchester and the class settled down to do excellent work on the heavy coal hauls from Wankie. In 1938 a further twelve examples came from the Manchester works and the augmented total enabled the 16s to operate additionally between Salisbury and Umtali and they easily lifted 700-ton freights over this route's 1 in 60 banks. When first acquired in 1929, a single 16 cost the R.R. £12,467 and the Company recently stated that the first engine, No. 600, had run over 1½ million miles prior to her withdrawal in the 1960s – the actual figure given was 1,621,994 miles! This engine now proudly resides in the Bulawayo Railway Museum and she is already regarded as an important national relic.

As their time expired on Rhodesia's main lines the 16s, unlike many engines, were not destined for the breaker's yard, as the first nine to be withdrawn were sold to the Benguela Railway, Angola, in 1963/4. The remainder survived for a while on the R.R. until most were purchased by Dunns Engineering of Witbank, South Africa, for refurbishing and resale to colliery companies. This was an excellent move upon Dunns' part as these Garratts were to prove highly suitable on the heavy slogging coal hauls frequently encountered in South African collieries. Thus the 16ths can now be seen in three different countries with almost the entire class remaining in existence, although at least one engine was broken up in Rhodesia and another had to be cannibalised by Dunns to obtain spare parts. Nevertheless, the remainder are still highly active and it is fascinating to think that some of these will soon be fifty years old!

Although no 16s work in Rhodesia today, their rather streamlined relations, the 16A 2–8–2 + 2–8–2, are very busy indeed, having come from Beyer Peacock between 1952 and 1953. These thirty 16As are exactly what they look – a more modern version of the 16, and dimensionally, the two classes are almost identical.

The engine shown belongs to the Transvaal Navigation Colliery, situated near Witbank, being one of the engines sold to Dunns Engineering. She is No. 609, an engine from the 1938 batch, and despite two changes of ownership since her R.R. days, the engine is still decked with her Rhodesian badge, initials and numberplate. No. 609 is represented making an all-out assault with a full tonnage for the Bezuidenhoutsrus exchange sidings some miles distant.

This occasion was a particularly memorable one for me, as No. 609 was the first Garratt engine I had seen for sixteen years and the memories she evoked were extremely vivid. Little did I know that when Britain's L.M.S. Garratts disappeared in the 1950s my next acquaintance with the type would be one frosty morning at a Transvaal colliery in 1973; coincidentally, the first 16s were being built at Beyer Peacock's works around the same time as the L.M.S. ones! Once again I heard the syncopated roar of a Garratt and after so long, it is small wonder that the occasion was the epitome of music and nostalgia. Of course, I was to see many subsequent Garratts whilst in Africa, but this first sighting was strangely beautiful, whereas the later ones were to be stimulating and exciting. What a picture this stately veteran made as she bellowed her way across the veld that winter's morning.

Watching No. 609 pass, I thought back to a rainy afternoon in 1953, when as children, a friend and I illicitly stole into Derby Locomotive Works. Gaining the Erecting Shop unseen, we eagerly disappeared inside, only to be stopped dead in our tracks by the sight which greeted us. Aghast we exchanged glances, for there confronting us were the squalid remains of two half-scrapped ex L.M.S. 2–6–0 + 0–6–2 Garratts. We were speechless, because at that time the Garratts were important main line freight engines in Britain and in those years of restricted steam scrappings this revelation came as an unexpected shock. So poignant was that occasion, that to this day I can still see the cut-up sheets of boiler plating and framing lying amid heaps of boiler lagging on the Erecting Shop floor, with the fragmented engines forlornly looming above. I still remember the two gloomy children who crept back over the Gasworks wall that afternoon and I also remember that when we got home and related our story no one would believe us! For some years longer we revered the sight of the surviving Garratts on the Midland main line until, by 1958, like a figment of childhood, they were gone.

R.R. Nos.	Builder	Date
600–607	Beyer Peacock	1929/30
608–619	Beyer Peacock	1938

Leading Dimensions

Cylinders (4)	$18\frac{1}{2}$ in. $\times$ 24 in.
Boiler pressure	180 lb per sq. in.
Driving wheel diameter	4 ft 0 in.
Grate area	$49\frac{1}{2}$ sq. ft
Tractive effort 85% b.p.	52,364 lb
Total weight f.w.o.	156 tons
Total length	81 ft 8 in.
Coal capacity	11 tons
Water capacity	Front tank: 3,340 gallons
	Rear tank: 1,850 gallons

Harold Edmonson once called these engines 'glamour girls' – hardly could a more appropriate title be found, for the 15th Class are indeed of feminine gender just as the R.R.'s 20th Class represents a stalwart masculinity. Their strange wheel arrangement of 4–6–4 + 4–6–4 is both different and pleasing, whilst the combination of large driving wheels and streamlined tanks engenders an extremely racy-looking engine. I am told that everyone who visits Rhodesia falls for these engines. The way they sensuously romp out from Bulawayo hugging the curves and spinning their large wheels is a lovely sight, whilst their capacity for speed is unequalled.

The initial four were delivered in 1940, shortly after the commencement of World War II and were intended to work the lonely 284 mile journey from Bulawayo to Mahalapye on the Mafeking line; a route which traverses the wild Botswana country. It is suggested that the 15ths' wheel arrangement was based upon a successful batch of similar Garratts delivered to Sudan during the late 1930s.

The immediate success of these four engines led the R.R. to adopt the class for general mixed traffic work and further examples were ordered after the war. By 1952 the R.R. possessed 74 and their high capacity for speed caused them to be known as 'Greyhounds' by Rhodesian crews. These engines undertook much work over the 303 miles between Salisbury and Bulawayo by operating 1,050-ton freight trains and 560-ton passenger/mail trains. These latter were whisked up to 50 m.p.h., the official speed maximum, though any Rhodesian engineman will admit that the 'Greyhounds' are capable of considerably more than this. Over many years they monopolised the Botswana line, which after 1966 was worked right through to Mafeking giving the 15s a 484 mile run, but nowadays their swansong is on the lines between Bulawayo/Gwelo and Bulawayo/Wankie/Victoria Falls, as the extremely poor water available in Botswana did terrible damage to their boilers and hastened the complete dieselisation of this route in 1973. Nearly always employed on long distance runs, the 15s have frequently attained monthly running figures of up to 10,000 miles! Nine are in Zambia, having been left there after the territorial split with Rhodesia, but it is doubtful that these engines are used very much today.

Chris Butcher informed me that he had recorded nine different detail variations on the 15ths, but the principal one was that the last forty engines built were classified 15A by virtue of a higher boiler pressure for greater tractive effort. These are set out below to their official nomenclature but their boilers have been swapped around indiscriminately; accordingly, no permanent differentiation can be made. The 1940 engines had a beautifully archaic-looking bunker design, whilst later engines received larger capacity semi-streamlined ones. Certainly these later ones accentuated the 'Greyhound' appeal, but the original design was most appealing. Two 15A boilers have been fitted with Giesl Ejectors over recent years and these have, in turn, appeared on various locomotives, but now both have been removed and no further action is envisaged. The 15A Garratt was beautifully commemorated on the 1/6d Rhodesian postage stamp as part of a special issue upon the seventieth anniversary of the Salisbury–Beira line.

Although in 1973 the Rhodesian steam age was fast drawing to a close, the scene at Bulawayo shed was nothing short of fantastic. It was here that Rhodesia's surviving steam fleet was concentrated and almost every engine was a Garratt: the sight truly rivalled the famous Masons Hill stud in Natal. The depot was literally teeming with Garratts – many being 15ths recently displaced from the Botswana line. A good many were spotless and despite their black livery much detail work was done out in red; almost without exception the entire fleet had come from Beyer Peacock of Manchester. As I stood watching this array of British achievement I could not help but think how the Garratt locomotive came into being and how Beyer Peacock took up the idea and unwittingly produced one of the world's most famous steam types and possibly the most exciting variation upon the 'conventional' locomotive ever known.

H. W. Garratt, who first conceived the principle, was an independent British engineer, and having perfected his design he took out a patent in 1907. Some years later Beyer Peacock of Gorton, Manchester, took up this innovation, without much initial enthusiasm, by building a 2 ft 0 in. gauge compound Garratt for Tasmania. But this was only a beginning, and soon the Company was to exploit the Garratt principle all over the world, their name becoming synonymous with it. I could not help but wonder what the directors of Beyer Peacock and Garratt himself would have thought, if in 1912, they could have glimpsed that depot in Bulawayo as it was to be sixty years later; the depot held four Garratt classes, 14A, 16A, 15 and 20, totalling over seventy engines, with hardly an orthodox locomotive in sight! I mention this especially because Garratt died shortly after Beyer Peacock accepted his patent and consequently he never knew the contribution he had made to steam locomotive engineering.

159

After visiting Bulawayo I went to see the 15s working the great coal hauls from the Wankie coalfield to Bulawayo – Rhodesia's last important steam duty. This epic 217-mile journey takes about thirteen hours and each train carries two crews which alternate duties; a caboose being provided in the train for sleeping and cooking en route.

Plate 38 depicts the numberplate of 15th Class No. 404, possibly Africa's most ill-fated locomotive. This engine arrived from Beyer Peacock in 1951 and within a few years she had acquired the reputation of being troublesome in a rather uncanny way by becoming continually involved in minor accidents. Initially her misdemeanours were of a mild nature, but later they graduated to more serious things and the engine began to cause deaths. She killed people on a level-crossing and killed again during a violent head-on collision in Botswana. No. 404 became known as 'The Mankiller'. History has frequently produced such cursed engines and railway folklore abounds with them, but few reflect the brooding dismality with which 404 was regarded by the engine crews. The climax came one night as she was working up to Wankie from Bulawayo, with one of the top Rhodesian drivers in charge. It was a night of inexplicable tragedy, for near Entuba were three tight curves over which speed was limited to some 20 m.p.h. On the night in question, it is estimated that 404 rode those curves at over 60 m.p.h. She violently held the first two before derailing on the third; the engine rolled over several times with the train piling up behind, the wrecked and half-buried engine came to rest 400 yards from the place of derailment. The driver was killed and the reason for the ridiculously high speed was never found out. However, this was enough; her numberplate was hoisted onto a tombstone improvised from sleepers; synonymously came the declaration that 404's days were over and, after a miraculous rebuilding in Bulawayo Works she was renumbered 424 in an effort to break the spell. I am told upon good authority that ever since this renumbering she has never so much as jumped a rail. Plate 5 shows the rebuilt and exorcised engine running as 424 during a wild moment at Matetsi, a small native village which is the final watering stop on the run up to Victoria Falls.

Number 424 is seen at Matetsi heading a coke train bound for Zaire and she took this up to Victoria Falls before handing over to the Zambian Railways. Her scheduled return working was the evening mail from Victoria Falls to Bulawayo, and later that day I had the pleasure of seeing her standing in the Falls station heading a marvellous rake of thirteen brown and cream clerestory coaches: a glamorous train with vintage appeal led by an immaculate semi-streamlined Garratt. As the passengers boarded the train amid the pre-departure bustle, the aroma of cooking dinners floated from the restaurant car and the tinkle of cups and plates could be heard in the buffet car; everything seemed so orderly and fine. But I considered the epitaph for a demon, which provided the grim testimony to this engine's past because her old numberplate still sat grotesquely up in the hills but a few miles distant. A chime whistle rang out over the Falls and with consummate ease the train glided away into the darkness, away under the spangled universe of a Rhodesian night to commence its long uneventful journey to Bulawayo.

Class	R.R. Nos.	Builder	Date
15	350–353	Beyer Peacock	1940
15	354–363	Beyer Peacock	1947/8
15	364–383	Beyer Peacock	1949
15A	384–413	Beyer Peacock	1949/50/51
15A	414–423	Franco-Belge	1952 (under licence from B.P.)
15A	424	Renumbered from 404	

Leading Dimensions

Cylinders (4)	$17\frac{1}{2}$ in. $\times$ 26 in.
Boiler pressure	180 lb per sq. in. (200 lb 15A)
Driving wheel diameter	4 ft 9 in.
Grate area	49·6 sq. ft
Tractive effort 85% b.p.	42,750 lb (47,496 lb 15A)
Total weight f.w.o.	187 tons
Total length	92 ft 4 in.
Coal capacity	$12\frac{1}{2}$ tons (majority)
Water capacity	Front tank: 4,250 gallons
	Rear tank: 2,750 gallons

R.R. 20 Class 4–8–2 + 2–8–4 Garratt   Plate No. 39

The Rhodesian Garratt saga, which began in 1926, was to end thirty-two years later when the last super-power 20th Class engines were delivered. Over those years the R.R. received 250 Garratt locomotives and in terms of mileage and traffic density few railways can ever have used the type so extensively. After the war, much heavier power was needed to operate the single track main line through Northern Rhodesia, especially the 107-mile Kafue–Broken Hill section which limited the Class 12 4–8–2s to 680 tons on account of its 1 in 64½ gradients. This line, which is now in Zambia, was extremely important in carrying southbound copper and chrome ore trains along with the northbound coal hauls from Wankie up to the Copper Belts. An engine was needed equivalent to a brace of 12s and thus capable of working 1,400-ton trains throughout. Accordingly, F. E. Hough, the R.R. Chief Mechanical Engineer, produced this 'pièce de résistance' of Rhodesian steam traction; an engine with the same driving wheel diameter as a 12th, but with over twice the tractive effort and within an axle loading of 17 tons. This was a greater axle weight than the 12s but by 1954, when the initial fifteen 20th Class were delivered, the R.R. had largely completed relaying their main lines with 80 lb rail. The new Garratts operated the heavy copper and coal hauls with relish, quickly clearing the backlog of tonnage which had built up for want of better motive power. They are the only R.R. engines fitted with mechanical stokers as their immense power necessitates a 63·1 sq. ft grate area.

Complete satisfaction with the 20s caused the R.R. to order a further 46 engines from Beyer Peacock. These arrived a few years later and although the first six were identical with the 1954 engines, the last forty were known as 20A, simply on account of their inner radial truck wheels being the same diameter as their bogie wheels!

This second order arrived at Beyer Peacock simultaneously with an S.A.R. request for GMAM Garratts – engines which the 20s are frequently likened to. Beyer Peacock could not cope with such a heavy demand for large engines and the Company got into difficulties, being forced to subcontract many GMAMs to the North British Co. These difficulties are often cited as being the reason for the firebox fractures which cursed the 20 Class – a fault absent from the GMAMs, despite their boiler design being similar! The Rhodesian Railways took action against Beyer Peacock on account of this trouble and the law suite was even perpetuated after the Company had gone out of business. Another serious problem which blighted the 20s was fractures in their bar frames and it was later regarded that had they been given the cast steel beds, as fitted to the GMAMs, this problem could have been avoided. In general the 20s have never matched the 15s' availability, as their smaller driving wheels set up more wear on the working parts.

Nevertheless, excellent performances have been given by these giants and they settled down to a monopoly of traffic operation over the Northern Rhodesian main line between Livingstone and Ndola on the Congo border, whilst other members of the class were allocated to Bulawayo. Two engines, rather strangely the first and last built, had to be scrapped owing to terrible accidents. One of these, No. 760, was extensively wrecked in a head-on collision with No. 726 at Magoyne in February 1963 and any salvageable parts from her had to be used to rebuild the almost equally ruined 726. This rebuilding, which began at Bulawayo Works in 1964, was seriously held up for want of a new boiler and straightening of the frames and both engines were nearly cut up, so impossible did the task seem; it was not until 1970 that No. 726 took the rails again! Certainly this is a long time-span over which to have an important engine out of operation but the condition of these two engines upon their arrival at Bulawayo Works could only be described as horrific.

By virtue of their superb hauling capacity, the 20s are credited with partly thwarting the case for electrification over the 303 mile Bulawayo–Salisbury and 207 mile Kafue–Nkana lines. After the division of Rhodesia's Railways with Zambia in June 1967, some forty-four 20s passed to the Zambian Railways where they remain today. Apart from those lost in accidents, the remaining Rhodesian engines are now ending their time between Bulawayo–Gwelo and Bulawayo–Wankie: upon these duties they work turnabout with the 15th Class, although when it comes to bringing the coals home from Wankie the 20th excels.

The picture shows a 20 getting away from Wankie and commencing the long haul to Bulawayo. She is featured passing a lineside Baobab tree in an effort to symbolise Rhodesia; for both are typical features of the bleached, sunny Rhodesian landscape.

Class	R.R. No.	Builder	Date
20	700–714	Beyer Peacock	1954
20	715–720	Beyer Peacock	1957
20A	721–760	Beyer Peacock	1957/8

Leading Dimensions
Cylinders (4)	20 in. × 26 in.
Boiler pressure	200 lb per sq. in.
Driving wheel diameter	4 ft 3 in.

Grate area	63·1 sq. ft
Tractive effort 85% b.p.	69,330 lb
Total weight f.w.o.	225 tons
Total length	95 ft
Coal capacity	14½ tons
Water capacity	Front tank: 5,450 gallons
	Rear tank: 2,550 gallons

RHODESIAN INDUSTRIAL: Wankie Colliery Co. 4–8–2 (R.R. 19 Class) (S.A.R. 19D Class) Plate No. 42

The lights over the darkened Wankie Coalfield fell into several principal groups, each denoting a mine and its related outbuildings. But as one looked towards Thompson Junction it was as if this whole area had been swallowed up, for not a light could be seen through the enveloping blackness. Yet it was from here that there came a heavy cough of exhaust and a harsh whistling: a train was on its way. The coughs settled down to a regular, laboured sequence and any thoughts that the train might have been a main liner heading out to Victoria Falls were banished when the angular shape of a green 19D engine came into sight with flaming droplets of incandescent fuel bouncing along underneath. She was heading a long string of empties back up to No. 2 Colliery. Vomiting flame, the big engine strove towards me, bearing the stress until, in a frenzied cacophony of despair, she slipped. A myriad of friction sparks from the rails were promptly dowsed by orange tinted jets of steam, as the sanding apparatus tried to arrest the affray. The outrage continued and flaming cinders flew upwards with incredible velocity, rivalling in brilliance their blanched relations which sedately looked down from the star-sown sky. Becoming akin to an ejaculating Roman Candle, the heavy engine found her feet at last and dug into the rails with renewed vigour. The fit was over, the waggons rolled steadily by, for the engine had now gained confidence as indeed one would expect, because this steeply graded industrial line was not worked by any vapid and archaic engine, but by one of the indefatigable 19D 4–8–2s – one of Africa's steam greats. This engine, proudly lettered WANKIE COLLIERY COMPANY LTD NO. 2 is illustrated as described.

Having forfeited the 19D to the maze of colliery sidings, I returned to my abode at the old Wankie Hotel, whose opalescence was just discernible upon the hillside above Old Wankie station. As I entered, the smoke-filled den proffered its usual air of gaiety; with the sound of music pounding and animated voices filling the air – such was the rough glamour of this coal/rail community. Wankie is steeped in atmosphere and history. Imagine a huge industrial complex suddenly looming up amid tracts of virgin land. Wankie is known world-wide for its game reserves and the surrounding terrain is both beautiful and unspoiled, but it was here that providence laid Rhodesia's coal and the much needed fruits of that pristine blessing are reaped today by four collieries. This is Rhodesia's only coalfield and over 220,000 tons of coal per month are transported away down the main line to Bulawayo in some ten Garratt-hauled trains per day. The fuel goes to thermal power stations throughout the country, also to steel works and industry in general. No. 1 Colliery and an odious coking plant formed from a fantastic tapestry of juxtaposed shapes, are situated immediately opposite the hotel, their purpose being to produce over 30,000 tons of coke per month. This whole complex is named after Wankie Thompson, an old pioneer who discovered the coalfield. The industry has recently been developed by Anglo-American but still trades under the name of Wankie Colliery Co. Wankie will always be remembered as the scene of possibly the worst mining disaster in history when 430 men were killed by an underground explosion, the mine in No. 2 Colliery where this happened now being sealed off as a communal grave.

Periodically, my room would become alive with a warm orange glow as if the entire place had suddenly ignited. This effect was not unpleasant for it was the glare of the adjacent coke ovens as they shot an orgy of flame skywards. When the hotel closed for the evening, Wankie with all its turbulence would collate some shreds of slumber; but even this was interjected by the appalling sounds issuing from the coke works which operated throughout twenty-four hours. Each night a Class 12 4–8–2 would come up from Thompson Junction to shunt these works, usually arriving some time before midnight. There is something comforting and reassuring about the sound of a shunting steam engine and never more so than with the 12s, their exhaust being so firm and melodious. Thompson Junction shed took great pride in these engines and maintained them in superb mechanical order, especially the valve settings which their exhausts clearly announced to be impeccable. Before the Garratts came to Rhodesia, the 12s were principal main line power; Thompson Junction retains four of these gems for local tripping and shunting: Nos. 175, 177, 187 and 190.

I heard the 12 come up that evening, and the quiet interval whilst she took water was followed by a lively bout of shunting. Sleeplessly I wandered out onto the verandah and looked over the industrial maze. I could have been in the heart of the Ruhr, yet not three miles across country, in the hostile surrounding bush, were elephants, giraffes, lions and the occasional lurking leopard. I could just discern the engine moving up and down through a sea of waggons, playfully buffetting them around the works with a series of clangs and sending them spinning off in all directions as if she were playing an enormous game of billiards. I followed her progress up and down the yard, noticing that each time the fireman added a round of coal to her fire a copper-shrouded inferno danced in her swirling smoke trails. It was now after 1.00 a.m. and Wankie had fallen to its precarious slumber; a slumber which would be rapidly swept away when the flux of early morning shift began! If rest was my emprise then it must be immediate, for neither man nor beast sleeps through the bedlam of the Wankie dawn. Hastened by both this sentiment and the chill air, I returned to my room soon to be lulled senseless by the continuing endeavours of engine No. 190.

The Wankie dawn is a majestic sight. The sun rises behind the industrial complex and slowly dissolves the blue misty haze. But before the vast flaming sky can truly beckon the new day, a long miraculous transition of form and tone must grace that industrial maze; a transition beginning with the delicacy of a water colour and ending with the firmness of an oil painting. As the sun dispenses the veiled mists its ever gaining dominance is met by a challenging vermillion blaze from the shrouded industry; a blaze so vivid as to diminish the benign sunlight not yet an hour born. But let another hour pass and see then who is master; let the sun soar but a few degrees. Then, the coke ovens can spit whatever angry and rebellious incandescence they will, for none will see it against that supreme luminary's all-enveloping effect.

But we were discussing 19Ds and belatedly I return to them, yet these engines are so inextricably bound with Wankie and its operations that I might be atoned for deviating into their environmental atmosphere. The Wankie engines are known as 19Ds because they are almost identical with the S.A.R.'s celebrated 19D class. Following the 19Ds' success in South Africa, the R.R. decided to order a batch of twenty similar engines from Henschel of Germany in 1951. At this time all rail operations throughout Wankie Colliery were operated by the R.R. at a cost of £50 per shunt, i.e. to take empties in and draw a loaded train out. The situation was intolerably uneconomical to the colliery company, especially as extensions in output were envisaged, and it was decided to tag four extra engines for Wankie Colliery onto the R.R.'s order. They cost the Company £47,000 each and were identical to the R.R. ones except they were given tenders from Class 12s, whilst their main line counterparts had huge, cylindrical, twelve-wheeled 'Torpedo' ones for long distance operations over the dry Botswana line. The only other difference to Wankie's engines was the absence of superheating elements, for it was regarded that the extra maintenance involved with these did not justify the benefits obtained over short distance running. Unlike their dour counterparts, the mine engines were done out in a delightful Brunswick Green and hand-somely lettered WANKIE COLLIERY COMPANY LTD. Today, two might be seen in steam simultaneously, on round the clock duties.

The 19s were the last 'conventional' engines ordered by the R.R. and brought to a close their long tradition of using the 4–8–2 as a standard basis for their straight engines. A later 19 was built as a condensing locomotive in 1954 and put to work over the Botswana line in an attempt to overcome water problems; one presumes that this was triggered off by the S.A.R.'s 25s, also introduced that year. She was known all over the system as 'Silent Suzie', but she was unpopular and after a collision the unhappy engine was rebuilt as a conventional 19 in 1958 and the R.R.'s projected experiments into condensing locomotives were taken no further.

These 4–8–2s are widely used on the S.A.R. and total some 337 locomotives if basic detail variations are included. Their classifications range from 19 to 19D, along with various reboilerings, and all, except the 19As, are almost identical dimensionally; they were built over the twenty-year period between 1928 and 1948. The 19D variant is by far the most numerous and can still be found operating secondary duties throughout the Republic.

Class	R.R. Nos.	Builder	Date
19	316–335	Henschel	1951/2 + 4 engines for Wankie Colliery
19B	337–338	Henschel	1952 Ex Rhokana Corp., Zambia
19C	336	Henschel	1954 'Silent Suzie'
19	1366–1369	Schwartzkopf	1928

Class	S.A.R. Nos.	Builder	Date
19A	675–710	S.L.M.	1929 (Smaller variant for lighter axle load)
19B	1401–1414	Schwartzkopf	1930
19C	2435–2484	North British	1935
19D	2506–2525	Krupp	1937
19D	2526–2545	Borsig	1937
19D	2626–2640	Skoda	1938
19D	2641–2680	Krupp	1938/9
19D	2681–2720	Borsig	1938/9
19D	2721–2770	Robert Stephenson & Co.	1945
19D	3321–3370	North British	1948

Leading Dimensions R.R. 19th/S.A.R. 19D

Cylinders	21 in. × 26 in.
Boiler pressure	200 lb per sq. in.
Driving wheel diameter	4 ft 6 in.
Grate area	36 sq. ft
Tractive effort 85% b.p.	36,090 lb
Total weight f.w.o.	With Class 12 tender: 134 tons
	With Torpedo tender: 157 tons
Total length	With Class 12 tender: 69 ft approx.
	With Torpedo tender: 86 ft 9 in.
Coal capacity	With Class 12 tender: 10 tons
	With Torpedo tender: 12 tons
Water capacity	With Class 12 tender: 4,250 gallons
	With Torpedo tender: 6,500 gallons

E.A.R. 59 Class 4–8–2 + 2–8–4 Garratt 'Mountains'
Plates Nos. 15, 35, 40

I took my place at breakfast on the terrace of Voi Game Lodge. The clouds were rolling in from the Indian Ocean and quickly subduing the watery sunshine of the inland coastal belt. Game was the predominant topic of conversation amongst visitors and whilst Game was also my concern, it was the metaphoric variety which interested me. My abode was carefully chosen, for the terrace overlooked the Mombasa–Nairobi line: a famous 332-mile stretch of railway which was host to the largest steam locomotives in the world today – the majestic 'Mountain' Class.

'Do you know that they still have steam trains here?' a loquacious American tourist announced to his companions. His friends greeted this revelation with a barrage of doubts, whereupon, raising his voice higher he cried, 'Yes, they do; I saw one only yesterday and quite a size it was too. All waggons you know, no people.' His group expressed more than a lethargic interest in this pronouncement, whereupon he promised to try to point one out to them. I proffered no information to the stranger, but he had obviously seen a 59, for they dominate this stretch of railway which, inland from Voi, skirts the edge of the great Tsavo Game Reserve.

This was a blissful time for me; I had already spent one marvellous day with the 59s. They move with the stealth and majesty of a lion – a swaggering mystical confidence indicative of immense power. The class is named after the highest mountains in East Africa; could any locomotive be more appropriately named than *Menengai Crater*, *Uluguru Mountains* or *Ol 'Donya Sabuk*? Such grandeur well befits them. The Tsavo Game Reserve is noted for its elephants – not to mention man-eating lions which still maraud in the area. Some forty miles to the north it is possible to see the world's largest steam engine taking water with the world's largest animal at Tsavo River where the 59s' water column is on a slight embankment above the river where elephants come to drink. This seemed the very crystallisation of David Shepherd's wonderful film *The Man who Loved Giants*, few would deny the similarity between these mammals and huge steam locomotives. The 'Mountain' Class are allowed to take 1,200 tons over this railway and trains coming up from Mombasa to Nairobi have to climb almost the equivalent of one mile in altitude; Nairobi being situated on a 5,000-foot plateau. This single track line includes 1 in 60 gradients and many crossing loops, but the 59s make the journey in twenty-two hours, this mammoth safari being undertaken by the two regular crews assigned to each locomotive. Crew changing points are situated at Voi and Makindu, so that on a round trip each crew has three shifts of duty – cabooses are included in the train to accommodate the men off duty. Voi is also an important oil/water stop on the main line, apart from being the connecting junction for Tanzania.

Having completed breakfast, I made my way down to the station to see the day's activities. A westbound train was in, headed by *Mount Suswa*, and I found the engine quenching her insatiable appetite from

169

both oil and water columns simultaneously, her Westinghouse pump spitting rhythmically. Though superficially quiescent, she was bursting with tension; I marvelled at her 104 ft length and huge 7 ft 6 in. diameter boiler, thinking as I did so, how the slender Giesl chimney suits these 59s as it gives them a more powerful, pugnacious and yet streamlined look – it is a perfect refinement. Just before departure *Mount Suswa* suddenly 'boiled up', white oil smoke swirled from her chimney and an ear splitting whistle scream rang out. The cylinder cocks squirted aggressively and, issuing mighty 'woomphs', she slowly eased forward causing a surging deluge of water to cascade down from the rear tank. Bathed in water and steam, the maroon giant moved away with various shades of light and dark exhaust flirting out of her chimney until, anticipating the 1 in 67 climb, her exhaust suddenly climaxed into an inky turmoil which quickly spread into a mushroom over Voi. Astonishing as this was, she trebled her efforts when the gradient was reached, blacker and thicker came the acrid palls from her chimney until both sunshine and train were completely lost in a black enveloping oil haze and all that could be heard was the engine's wuthering, frenzied attack on the bank. Never before had I seen a locomotive throw up such an exhaust. But the tempest was far from over; crowning all her previous efforts came the most appallingly freakish mushroom of smoke as if the engine's oil tank itself had ignited in one terrible explosion – never had I seen such atomic vigour! The brooding discontent with which that smoke hung over Voi long after the train had gone was equalled only by the ominousness of the surrounding mountains.

I was later to discover the cause of that final outrage. It was the 'sanding treatment', whereupon the crew throw buckets of sand into the engine's firebox. This has the effect of cleaning the inner deposit of soot and carbon from the boiler tubes and ejecting it into the atmosphere; if such deposits were allowed to solidify they would obviously impair steaming. The E.A.R. rule book advises tube sanding to be undertaken every twenty miles or so, especially when the engine is working upgrade, but I could little imagine that *Mount Suswa*'s tubes had been done within twenty miles!

After an exciting day with the 'Mountains', 'Governors' and 'Tribals' – the engines which frequent Voi, I returned to the wooden lodge. From the terrace I watched the sun covering the hills with a counterpane of light shadow – azure twilight was slowly advancing. Up above a flock of hawks was circling effortlessly, adding a gentle

170

rippling momentum to the evening's stillness and the valley seemed
to radiate an all-pervading harmony. A whistle came from below as a
red Garratt distantly rolled into sight snaking its long silver box
freight across the valley floor. A red backing on her nameplate was
just visible; this was *Mount Kilimanjaro* heading for Mombasa. There
are times when Kenya comes close to the tourist brochure claim:
'God's own Paradise'.

The picture called 'Nairobi bound' indicates the predominant
greenness of Kenya's coastal belt as for some miles inland the rainfall
is heavy. How I remember a wet morning at Miritini, a small crossing
situated in a grove of palm trees eight miles inland from Mombasa.
The grey skies released a torrential deluge which had the appearance
of lasting all day. Gloomily I sat under the station awning, watching
the raindrops hammering onto the earth and, following the course of
a thousand mighty rivers and eternal swamp, I beheld the land of Noah.
Eventually an eastbound was signalled through the station, breaking a
lull of almost four hours. Soon the characteristically red shape of
Mount Shengena approached, cutting vividly through the green surrounds, whilst her flickering orange fireglow provided a welcome
highlight on this shrouded grey morning. As the Garratt approached
at speed, the Station Controller dashed out wearing a tarpaulin and
tropical rain hat to hand the engine's crew a huge wicker tablet which
allowed them to continue into the next section. As the engine passed, a
young barefoot African girl suddenly darted out into the deluge and,
standing not ten feet from the track, she began to dance vigorously to
the rhythms of the heavy rumbling waggons. Her soaked dress showed
every movement of her lithe body, as her skinny legs mimicked the
pulsating train. After a few waggons had passed, a boy ran out to join
her, and the pair danced frenziedly: it was like the finest performance
from a wild gipsy carnival. The percussive waggons rolled endlessly,
as it was a long train of empties for Mombasa, and not until the
caboose had passed by did the children stop dancing. Then, turning
her back upon the boy, the glamorously scruffy hoyden made off
through the trees. I had witnessed a wonderful facet of African life –
a distant whistle from the train completed the performance.

171

bearings; in accordance with E.A.R. policy the entire class was built to burn oil. The Mombasa–Nairobi line is the busiest in East Africa, being laid throughout with the 95 lb rail necessary to accommodate the 59s' 21 ton axle loading. It seems hardly believable that the E.A.R. would wish for anything bigger than a 59, but a 372-ton 4–8–4 + 4–8–4 Garratt, with a 26-ton axle load and little short of half as big again as a 59, did reach the drawing board stage. These were to be the 61 Class, but tragically they were never to see light of day; partly because of the 59s' enormous success and partly because of the E.A.R.'s increasing awareness of diesel traction – to which they are committed today. However, 61s or not, these 'Mountain' Class Garratts constitute one of the most sumptuous steam classes of all time.

E.A.R. Nos.	Builder	Date
5901–5934	Beyer Peacock	1955

Leading Dimensions

Cylinders (4)	20½ in. × 28 in.
Boiler pressure	225 lb per sq. in.
Driving wheel diameter	4 ft 6 in.
Grate area	72 sq. ft
Tractive effort 85% b.p.	83,350 lb
Total length	104 ft
Total weight f.w.o.	252 tons
Oil capacity	2,700 gallons
Water capacity	Front tank: 5,550 gallons
	Rear tank: 3,050 gallons

E.A.R. 60 Class 4–8–2 + 2–8–4 Garratt 'Governor'   Plate No. 46

What a glorious engine this chocolate-coloured Garratt is and what a lovely sight she makes daily plying her way along the frail Voi–Moshi line which links Kenya with Tanzania. With a business-like air, which seems intrinsic to these 'Governors', she fussily shunted the intermediate stations, her breathlessly silent Giesl exhaust being well augmented by four spitting cylinder cocks, combined with a multitude of inordinate interior gurglings and an anxious panting from her brake pumps – not to mention her curious high-pitched whistle, which sounded more like a nervous shriek than a locomotive. All East African locomotives are supposed to be maroon, but this engine's livery constitutes a hybridised version, for things do not always work out as intended, and it seems that frequent shortages of paint often necessitate the intermixing of 'foreign' colours: I don't think the E.A.R. get much further from maroon than chocolate, but they are capable of producing many chromatic variations between the two!

Known colloquially as 'Governors', the entire class was once named after the British Governors who controlled Kenya, Uganda and Tanganyika. After independence, it appeared that these commemorations were offensive to the new authorities and the railway management were instructed to have the names removed. Furthermore, the first engine was renamed *Umoja* – freedom! An idea was kindled to substitute the names of East African animals in lieu of the British personages, but this was never undertaken and it is almost certainly too late now. These were the Governors' names:

6001	*Sir Geoffrey Archer*	6016	*Sir Henry Moore*
6002	*Sir Hesketh Bell*	6017	*Sir John Hall*
6003	*Sir Stewart Symes*	6018	*Sir Charles Dundas*
6004	*Sir Frederick Jackson*	6019	*Sir Phillip Mitchell*
6005	*Sir Bernard Bourdillon*	6020	*Sir Evelyn Baring*
6006	*Sir Harold MacMichael*	6021	*Sir William Gowers*
6007	*Sir Mark Young*	6022	*Sir Andrew Cohen*
6008	*Sir Wilfred Jackson*	6023	*Sir Edward Northey*
6009	*Sir Edward Twining*	6024	*Sir James Hayes-Sadler*
6010	*Sir Donald Cameron*	6025	*Sir Henry Colville*
6011	*Sir William Battershill*	6026	*Sir Horace Byatt*
6012	*Sir Percy Girouard*	6027	*Sir Gerald Portal*
6013	*Sir Henry Belfield*	6028	*Sir H. Johnston*
6014	*Sir Joseph Byrne*	6029	*Sir Edward Grigg*
6015	*Sir Robert Brooke-Popham*		

This picture shows No. 6024 musing its way towards Voi with an overnight mixed freight from Moshi, a town beneath Mount Kilimanjaro, in Tanzania. Filmed in the early Kenyan light, this study is a particular favourite of mine. If I might discuss it objectively, my aim was to produce a stimulating geometrical design. Having used the two strong verticals to make an interaction between the subject and its related signal, the outline of the background hills was then set tantalisingly below the half-way mark of the format, adding valuable

Many 59s have Sikh drivers, the most famous example being 5918, *Mount Gelai* – a brass plate from this engine's cab is sketched below. The overall condition of *Mount Gelai* is possibly unrivalled anywhere in the world today. Her cab interior is more akin to a Sikh Temple than a locomotive footplate for its boiler face abounds in polished brasswork, embellished with mirrors, clocks, silver buckets and a linoleum floor. The crews are known throughout East Africa as the 'Magnificent Foursome' and so well do they care for their steed, that a failure is almost unknown and no breakdown in traffic has ever been recorded against this engine since they took over ten years ago. She has the highest mileage record between shoppings and on several occasions 5918 has been taken to Nairobi Works for overhaul as a matter of policy, rather than for any recognisable necessity!

Twenty 'Mountains' are allocated to Nairobi, whilst the remaining fourteen belong to Mombasa. The Mombasa engines can be easily picked out by their black backed number and name plates, compared with Nairobi's red ones. How these engines are revered by crews and engineers alike; little inducement being needed to evoke an enthusiastic discussion. The following fragment from my conversation with a locomotive fitter at Mombasa will convey the spirit – such were his phrases. . . . 'Yes, 5931 is the cleanest, but then she's only been out of shops a month – and with the official maroon livery too. 5913 is chocolate brown – she belongs to Nairobi. They say that 5912 is the best – that's the one with wing plates on the smokebox, I've heard tales that she will go up Miritini bank with a full load at fifteen per cent cut off – but I doubt it. 5906 has a cracked frame and one of her drivers is acting day foreman here whilst his engine is in Nairobi shops. The one that always gets the limelight is 5918, but you know about her. I agree, the names are impressive, personally I like *Ol 'Donya Sabuk* – she's one of ours, we have her in the sick bay at present, you've possibly seen her. Did you hear about 5917 hitting a herd of elephants last week?' I hope such lyrical phrases as these convey something of the spirit; to me they almost constitute a style of free form poetry. Here is the 59 Class:

5901	*Mount Kenya*	5918	*Mount Gelai*
5902	*Ruwenzori Mountains*	5919	*Mount Lengai*
5903	*Mount Meru*	5920	*Mount Mbeya*
5904	*Mount Elgon*	5921	*Mount Nyiru*
5905	*Mount Muhavura*	5922	*Mount Blackett*
5906	*Mount Sattima*	5923	*Mount Longonot*
5907	*Mount Kinangop*	5924	*Mount Eburu*
5908	*Mount Loolmalasin*	5925	*Mount Monduli*
5909	*Mount Mgahinga*	5926	*Mount Kimhandu*
5910	*Mount Hanang*	5927	*Mount Tinderet*
5911	*Mount Sekerri*	5928	*Mount Kilimanjaro*
5912	*Mount Oldeani*	5929	*Mount Longido*
5913	*Mount Debasien*	5930	*Mount Shengena*
5914	*Mount Londiani*	5931	*Uluguru Mountains*
5915	*Mount Mtorwi*	5932	*Ol 'Donya Sabuk*
5916	*Mount Rungwe*	5933	*Mount Suswa*
5917	*Mount Kitumbeine*	5934	*Menengai Crater*

The 'Mountains' were among the final steam engines delivered to East Africa, having been ordered in 1950 to cope with the ever-increasing import/export traffic on the Mombasa–Nairobi section of the Kenya–Uganda main line. Inadequate motive power had created a serious backlog of freight, necessitating new and dynamic locomotives. Owing to the huge demand for Garratt engines, resulting from an upsurge in traffic after the war, it was impossible for Beyer Peacock to deliver the 59s until 1955. When finally delivered, the 'Mountains' proved superb and even today many E.A.R. officials believe their performances, both operational and economic, to be superior to diesel locomotives. Certainly the 'Mountains' consumed less fuel and water per ton mile than any other East African steam design. They are conventionally built on bar frames and all axles have roller tension. Furthermore, I tried to accentuate the lovely feeling of distance conjured up by looking from the priceless splash of russet around the signal's base, through to the beginning of the distant hills. This feeling of space is a cornerstone of landscape pictorialism, both in portraying the illusion of naturalism and also psychologically, for perspective is like an open gate which lures us away from the troubled foreground of the world.

The 'Governors' had the distinction of being the first E.A.R. class to acquire this magnificent maroon livery: a colour once used by the Tanganyika Railway and later adopted as standard after the railways united in 1948. In appearance, the 60s are like a small 59, or as otherwise described, like a 59 growing up! The similarity is almost certainly accentuated by the Giesl chimneys, which, along with the engine's livery, provides a unique aspect of East African Garratts. A direct descendant from the earlier 56 Class, the 'Governors' were delivered with standard chimneys and the metamorphosis of Gieslising was largely influenced by the celebrated railway author A. E. Durrant who, as a professional engineer, moved from Swindon to the E.A.R. drawing office in Nairobi in 1955. Durrant, after corresponding with Dr Giesl-Gieslingen in Vienna, arranged for the East African Railways C.M.E., Willie Bulman, to be given full information of the Giesl apparatus and in 1957, a Giesl chimney was fitted experimentally to a 'Governor'. The results were satisfactory and after further tests, a full-scale conversion of almost the entire East African steam fleet was undertaken. A significant reduction in fuel consumption was obtained, but perhaps more important, was the increase in power achieved by reducing the cylinder back-pressure. However, both improvements were highly beneficial, especially when one considers the long, heavy runs undertaken by East African engines.

The 'Governors' have, over many years, been the standard light-weight Garratt of East Africa, for they possess a remarkably light 11 ton axle loading – compared with the 21 tons of a 59 Class! They have done good service in all three countries, but especially over the Dar-es-Salaam to Morogoro section on the Tanganyika Central Line and the Kampala to Torora line in Uganda. Today many are at Moshi and from here they work to Voi, Tanga and Arusha. The 'Governors', in company with the 59s, are now the only surviving East African Garratt locomotives.

E.A.R. Nos.	Builder	Date
6001–6012	Franco-Belge, Paris	1954
(built under licence from Beyer Peacock)		
6013–6029	Beyer Peacock	1954

Leading Dimensions

Cylinders (4)	16 in. × 24 in.
Boiler pressure	200 lb per sq. in.
Driving wheel diameter	4 ft 0 in.
Grate area	48·75 sq. ft
Tractive effort 85% b.p.	43,520 lb
Total length	90 ft
Total weight f.w.o.	152 tons
Oil capacity	1,800 gallons
Water capacity	Front tank: 3,038 gallons
	Rear tank: 1,574 gallons

E.A.R. 30/31 Classes 2–8–4 'Tribals' Plates Nos. 7, 48

'Kilimanjaro: though the Germans once courted you into their territory you behaved then as now, shamefully veiling your beauty with cloud. Your capricious moods, though accepted by Arusha's inhabitants, bitterly vex the thousands lured by the qualities of your winsome ways into travelling miles to see the dignity of your wild grandeur,' so thought I, as I passed Africa's highest mountain cloaked in obscurity. But, unheeding Kilimanjaro's ill-temper, I journeyed on. It was a long safari taking me from Nairobi – the nerve centre of East Africa – to Tabora, a distance of over 400 miles. Possibly I had been foolish to undertake the trip alone and by road, for the surface was little better than a cart track, whilst the country was often desolate, much of it unchanged since the advent of man. Driving was difficult, my vehicle became a raging bronco, stones continually pounded the underside, and a hideous phantom of dust pursued me every inch of the way. Violent though the iron-baked earth was, I rejoiced that this was not the wet season, because then a complete metamorphosis occurs: the road becomes a streaming quagmire quickly forbidding any passage. But I had good incentive to suffer such a journey because Tabora, though an isolated Tanzanian town, was one of East Africa's last important outposts for steam traction.

Nightfall was fast overtaking me as I reached the shanty town of

Babati. In this place of vegetables, scattering chickens, bustling women and hand carts my vehicle seemed out of place, but I had to remain there until morning. Having obtained a room in a decrepit oil-lit boarding house, I was offered chicken and rice. This provided good sustenance but it gave me the harrowing thought that the creature would be killed to order, so impoverished did the whole place seem. As I waited for that meal, I imagined the chef chasing the nearest chicken up the main street! During the evening, a motley assortment of half-wrecked buses arrived hell-bent on various over-land journeys as the nearest railheads were Arusha, Dodoma or Tabora – this last lying a tantalising 240 miles to the west!

I left the following morning at first light. My journey was un-deniably thrilling, but totally exhausting, as each gyration the vehicle took wrenched my nervous system with it; the effect being not unlike driving at speed on flat tyres. Africans of various tribes were passed en route; some out hunting with bows and arrows. By noon, I left the hilly country and descended onto a vast plateau which opened up for countless miles around. Far ahead across this tableland lay Tabora, served by the railway which ran from the coast at Dar-es-Salaam to Mwanza on Lake Victoria's shores. Under benign skies flecked with bobbled cloud I continued, until after eleven hours' driving, I finally reached my destination. Acutely exhausted and with a desultory mind, I made for the engine sheds in order to gain the prizes which would reward my pains.

A smiling array of red engines peeped from the German-built half roundhouse. My prizes, in order of presentation were: a 2–6–2T from Bagnalls of Stafford, a British-built 4–8–0 from fifty years ago, British 2–8–2s for ultra-light branch line work and, of course, the 'Tribals' – all three varieties standing side by side. These are the standard East African mixed traffic engines, handsome, modern and utilitarian in every way. Over one hundred were built for service throughout Kenya, Uganda and Tanzania. So began my adventure in Tabora; a place where the steam age reigns supreme, echoing its sounds by night and day over the dry, surrounding landscape.

Tabora's significance as a railway junction may be seen in the various routes radiating from it. The main line, already referred to, is simply known as the north line up to Mwanza and the south line in the Dar-es-Salaam direction. Additionally, there is the west line which splits at Kaliua, 76 miles out from Tabora: one section going westwards to Kigoma on Lake Tanganyika, 251 miles from Tabora;

the other running 207 miles south-west, to a little town called Mpanda, set in an isolated region completely reliant upon the railway. All routes have steam workings, especially the north and west ones; 'Tribals' predominate, but older classes have to be maintained for the ultra-light Mpanda section. Traffic was not heavy around Tabora, but with four routes there was always sufficient to sustain continued interest and, apart from the satisfying variety of motive power, where else can one see a maroon-coloured fleet of main line engines, many named, and some with a British pre-grouping character? I lament the scarcity of coloured and named engines in the world today, so the personality and variety of E.A.R. engines came as a true delight. Much of the East African system is rather rustic and charming, with many main lines being more akin to meandering lonely branches. But not all are like this, as those who like their drama a little more highbrow can always see the 'Mountain' Class Garratts working between Mombasa and Nairobi.

Each day at Tabora was like the unfolding of a variety performance; the separate acts following a pre-determined order, but each set against a different backcloth depending upon the train's route. But the top of the bill came at six o'clock when the overnight Mwanza Mail departed behind a 'Tribal'. Follow my description. About 5.30 each afternoon a gleaming maroon 'Tribal' backs onto the mail train comprised of eleven freshly painted chocolate and cream coaches. This is the big train of the day and it is always accompanied by a fully appropriate bustle throughout the station. The gentle evening sun lights the stage, as ceremoniously the superb maroon engine departs, perhaps *Jonam*, *Jopadhola* or *Kakwa* – one of Tabora's 31 Class, anyway. An ecstatic dark haze curls from the engine's chimney, steam shoots from her valves: both mingle with the pale blue sky. Now superimpose the colour of this train onto a green and orange land-scape, and you will envisage the 'Tribals' 'finest hour'.

Still borne by imagination's wings see the southbound mail leave Mwanza at almost the same hour; colourfully winding its way past Lake Victoria's shores. The 'Tribal's' exhaust drifts effortlessly over the water and as she whistles her way through the rocky fastness, her cry is echoed by a Lake steamboat sedately leaving the quayside bound for Kampala.

From a hillside above town I witnessed such a scene as this. Looking down on the lake through a gauze of trees, I followed the ship's movement over the water, a light breeze painted its progress in smoke. The shimmering water, the gently fluttering poplar trees, the graceful boat and westering sunlight all belonged to the golden sunlit world of Monet. The complementary hues of that Parisienne bliss indelibly etched themselves onto my mind. My eyes focussed to impressionism.

As a stud of engines, the 'Tribals' form the backbone of East African steam power, and perform mixed traffic work throughout the system. Some discussion of them may thus be timely. The original engines were the 29 Class for operating over the Kenya–Uganda main line on secondary and pick-up turns; the engines' design being based upon the Nigerian Railway's 'River' Class. The 29s differ from the two later variants in being 2–8–2s and a few years later the 30 Class appeared with a four-wheeled Delta truck to give better weight distribution. These engines, built for the Tanganyika central line, were given special 7,000 gallon tenders for working long distances through the dry interior regions. The 30s' tenders are interesting because they are carried on two six-wheel cast steel bogies incorporating shock-absorbers instead of springs! Both classes have a wide range of standard parts and an axle load of 13 tons. Simultaneously with the 30s came the slightly smaller 31 Class, with an $11\frac{1}{2}$ ton axle loading intended for use on the very lightly laid lines in Kenya and Uganda, especially those up to Thompson Falls, Nanyuki and Kasese. This is an extremely light axle weight for a relatively large engine, and great care has to be taken in handling these locomotives if persistent slipping bouts are to be avoided. Known collectively as the 'Tribals', the three classes are named after East Africa's largest tribes.

Notice their high running plate, long Giesl chimneys, cow catchers and rectangular brass nameplates. Their wonderfully evocative selection of tribal names rather reminds me of the colourful diversity found on the old L.M.S. 'Jubilee' Class. Here are the names and classes:

29 Class

2901	*Boran*	2917	*Kisii*
2902	*Bukusu*	2918	*Luo*
2903	*Bunyone*	2919	*Maragoli*
2904	*Chuka*	2920	*Marakwet*
2905	*Digo*	2921	*Masai of Kenya*
2906	*Dorobo*	2922	*Meru of Kenya*
2907	*Duruma*	2923	*Mogodo*

2908	Elgeyo	2924	Nandi
2909	Embu	2925	Nyika
2910	Galla	2926	Samburu
2911	Giryama	2927	Suk
2912	Kakamega	2928	Taveta
2913	Kamasia	2929	Teita
2914	Kamba	2930	Tiriki
2915	Kikuyu	2931	Turkana
2916	Kipsigis		

30 Class

*3001	Tanganyika	3014	Masai of Tanganyika
3002	Bena	3015	Meru of Tanganyika
3003	Bondei	3016	Mwera
3004	Chagga	3017	Ngindo
3005	Gogo	3018	Nyakyusa
3006	Ha	3019	Nyamwezi
3007	Haya	3020	Nyaturu
3008	Hehe	3021	Pare
3009	Iramba	3022	Pogoro
3010	Irakw	3023	Sambaa
3011	Luguru	3024	Sukuma
3012	Makonde	3025	Zaramo
3013	Makua	3026	Zigua

*Formerly Arusha

31 Class

3101	Baganda	3124	Chope
3102	Batoro	3125	Dodoth
*3103	Uganda	3126	Jie
3104	Alur	3127	Jonam
3105	Bagisu	3128	Jopadhola
3106	Bagwe	3129	Kakwa
3107	Bagwere	3130	Karamojong
3108	Bahehe	3131	Kenyi
3109	Bahororo	3132	Kumam
3110	Bakiga	3133	Lango
3111	Bakoki	3134	Lugbara
3112	Bakonjo	3135	Madi
3113	Bamba	3136	Sebei

181

3114	*Banyala*		3137	*Iteso*
3115	*Banyankore*		3138	*Upe*
3116	*Banyaruanda*		3139	*Pokomo*
3117	*Banyoro*		3140	*Rendille*
3118	*Banyuli*		3141	*Ribe*
3119	*Basamia*		3142	*Sanye*
3120	*Basese*		3143	*Somal*
3121	*Basoga*		3144	*Tharaka*
3122	*Batwa*		3145	*Tsoto*
3123	*Bavuma*		3146	*Wamia*

*Formerly *Acholi*

MASAI OF TANGANYIKA

E.A.R. Nos.	Builder	Date
29 Class		
2901–2902	North British	1951
2903–2920	North British	1952
2921–2931	North British	1955
30 Class		
3001–3014	North British	1955
3015–3026	North British	1956
31 Class		
3101–3127	Vulcan Foundry, Lancs	1955
3128–3146	Vulcan Foundry, Lancs	1956

Leading Dimensions

Cylinders	18 in. × 26 in. (31: 17 in. × 26 in.)
Boiler pressure	200 lb per sq. in.
Driving wheel diameter	4 ft 0 in.
Grate area	38 sq. ft (31: 30 sq. ft)
Tractive effort 85% b.p.	29,835 lb (31: 26,600 lb)
Total length	29: 67½ ft; 30: 74½ ft; 31: 62½ ft
Total weight f.w.o.	29: 127 tons; 30: 144 tons; 31: 116 tons
Oil capacity	29: 2,056 gallons; 30: 1,950 gallons; 31: 1,667 gallons
Water capacity	29: 4,800 gallons; 30: 7,000 gallons; 31: 4,108 gallons

The real adventure at Tabora came when the E.A.R. provided me with an inspection car for a two-day trip over the remote line up to Mpanda which lay 207 miles distant across arid, tangled scrub country infested with tsetse flies. Sometimes less than three trains per week make this journey, whilst in winter, services often have to be abandoned as the 43 lb track frequently washes away; especially on sections laid without ballast. During these times of danger, waggons are sometimes pushed ahead of the locomotive in case the track should give way, so affording the engine some chance to survive. Even throughout the dry season, speed is restricted to 15 m.p.h. over many stretches. Laid over very recent years, this line serves isolated communities with water during the dry season, but its principal function is to service Mpanda's mining interests: these are chiefly gold mines though some lead mines also occur. The E.A.R. have attempted to close down the route on many occasions, but the government will not allow this, and accordingly the state pays a percentage towards this grossly un-economic line's upkeep, because 130 miles of railway have to be specially maintained for this unusually light traffic, the area for miles around Mpanda being almost completely devoid of roads.

East African Railway's Inspection Car No. 89 was duly assembled into the Friday evening freight and I took possession earlier that afternoon. These British-built cars are used to carry officials making visits over the system and are equipped with study, kitchen, bathroom, shower, bedroom and toilet – everything that could be required for a long safari into remote areas. Eagerly I stowed away my belongings, including some special packs of food obtained in town and, having set out the coach to my liking, I went up to the engine sheds. Here, I was informed that locomotive 2611 was to be my engine: she was an ugly, scruffy, down-at-heel 2–8–2 from Bagnalls of Stafford. Entering the roundhouse, I found 2611 being prepared for the safari and a fitter, learning the nature of my interest in her, peered up from the inspection pit and, with an oily countenance, said, 'You'll be lucky to get back with this one – she's in a shocking state, we wouldn't mind if she rolled over into Ugalla River – we keep hoping!' Unable to share such sentiments, I found 2611's personality captivating; her British thoroughbred lines being distorted by Giesl chimney, Weir feed water heater and pumps, along with a large air-brake cylinder. She was a last survivor of the officially obsolete Tanganyika Railways M.L. class having been specially retained on account of her $9\frac{3}{4}$ ton axle load, in order to work the Mpanda line. Certainly the engine was a real 'Crate' and it was by this name that I came to know her.

We were scheduled away at five-thirty that afternoon, but well before this time 'The Crate' had coupled up to a 28-waggon freight train totalling 488 tons. A delay caused by a faulty brake pipe meant that we were not ready until nearly six o'clock, by which time we were forced to wait until the Mwanza Mail had departed. Locking up my I.C., I joined the engine. The Mail stood several tracks away behind 'Tribal' class 3129 *Kakwa*, and my driver, pointing to the engine, said, 'That's the tribe that General Amin of Uganda came from!' The mail departed as magnificently as ever, its chocolate coaches crammed with humanity of all kinds and after its receding exhaust had melted into the evening sky, we gained the peg: my adventure had begun. After a short tantrum of slipping, 'The Crate' picked up its train and rattled it out of Tabora: away through the evening towards the now golden west.

However humble the engine, there is something deeply exhilarating about footplate riding; when on a steam engine you belong with the privileged few; high as the pulpit and lofty as the throne is this high seat of man's aspirations. These were my thoughts as we gained speed, not that I regarded 2611 as humble, for already my affection was boundless and the engine my heroine! Soon Tabora faded into the arid waste and apart from the odd African village we passed into virgin bush; 2611's anguished roar became the pulse of Africa and sole companion of the now purple twilight.

It was dark when we reached our first stop at Mabama and here we passed 'Tribal' engine 3018 *Nyakyusa* bringing goods up from Kigoma, as the two routes are shared over the first sixty miles. Whilst 'The Crate' took water, I looked into the thatched African village to watch the women pounding maize with poles around a large wood fire set in the village square. Their swarthy bodies swayed rhythmically in the dancing firelight. The lovely tinge of wood smoke, combined with the earthy scent of the wild, produced a glorious aroma and when this mixed with the hot, oily emanations from 2611, the resulting effect was ecstatic. Soon we were off into the night, each mile taking us into increasingly wild country. For a time, the fires of African villages could be discerned, but these became less frequent, until blackness took command, relieved only by the engine's yellow glow bathing the tracksides like molten steel and revealing foxes and hyenas gaping incredulously at man's intrusion of their domain.

The liaison between driver and fireman was interesting to watch, as each time the driver made an adjustment to either regulator or valve setting, his fireman responded with the oil jets, ascertaining as he did so, the fire's condition by looking through the peep-hole in the firebox mouth. The atmosphere when travelling on an oil-burning locomotive is quite unusual, there being little footplate activity as the fireman can conduct most operations whilst seated. One misses the familiar clanging shovel and continually opening firehole doors.

After the junction, I bade the crew goodnight and returned to my I.C. Spreading my map across the table I studied our route and simultaneously undid one of my food packs. It was nearly midnight before I finished the meal and though exhausted with excitement, I was unable to turn my attentions to sleep. The coach grumbled and rolled along, periodically threatening to displace all contents onto the floor. Speed had now fallen drastically, the track was getting rougher, and the friendly companionship of the Kigoma line lay far behind. A black stare mocked my quest for recognition as I peered from the windows and I felt a strange emotion of loneliness. Where before had I ever known such desolation and isolation from my fellow beings? Tempered as these thoughts were by 'The Crate's' wheezing exhaust some waggon lengths ahead, I felt as if I were kneeling at the shrine of eternity.

About half-past one, our speed fell to walking pace: we had hit an arduous bank. 2611 was in agony. Now the track was so rough that I could hardly believe my coach was still on rails: it could have been running over the track bed. I opened my coach door but nothing answered, it was as if the whole of civilisation had been but an illusion. The hostile, unyielding landscape taunted me to succour from it whatever contentment I might. With what brazen helplessness could I face this expanse, when every implement of my intelligence had been wrought in civilisation's foundry: galvanised by the light of others? What talent could I proffer in this pristine circumstance? Cast now like a rivet falling from an ocean-going ship, I must inevitably sink to the havens of murky obscurity; the entrails of fate having led me thus far, were now to abandon me completely. But I was not destined to be alone: beasts crept from the night, now my equal and true companions, though I could not and would not befriend them, for they only made me yearn more for that civilisation which once degraded them to a bitter subordination. What sombre illusions were these; does not light penetrate even the darkest of dreams: was every

185

sensation financed from the coffers of hell? It was none of these things; I only suffered the pains of my idle remove from creation; my crippled dependence upon humanity: I had forgotten the story of Genesis. 'The Crate' wailed on as the petrification of that abstract night turned to a wonderous aura: it was almost three before I took to a partial sleep.

Sunrise brought a kinder Genesis: the delicate shrouds of light poured like cascading water into the leafy woodlands through which we now passed. These woodlands from time immemorial, shimmering in the early glaze of dawn, were as wonderous a start to a day as I have ever known. We travelled on, but I had no knowledge of our distance from Mpanda, except that the journey had been slow and laboured. I breakfasted quickly, intending to join the engine if we stopped again. Some miles later we paused to give water to a shambled shanty town of dwellings, and despite the early hour, all villagers swarmed around our train. Opening my door to dismount, I was greeted by a sea of blank faces. In Tabora these would have soon crystallised into friendliness, but here anything untoward was greeted with a bland amazement.

'Morning, how have you slept?' called a figure leaning from the engine. To my faintest grimace he retorted, 'Oh, those coaches are a thing you've really got to be accustomed to,' whereupon he disappeared inside the cab to turn off 2611's injector. We were still some two hours from Mpanda and our progress was continually interrupted to deliver water for the most remarkably isolated human settlements imaginable. I was enchanted by the big game we sighted; the animals freely living in these roadless tracts of land. The water stops provided us an opportunity to check 'The Crate's' motion, because the track was so poor that moving parts would suddenly work loose with very little warning. The rails were laid in fifteen- or thirty-foot lengths; much of it of German origin dating back to 1912.

At nine o'clock we finally reached Mpanda, a scattered conglomeration of buildings and dwellings stuck onto the landscape as if by glue. After depositing out train, 'The Crate' began to shunt, but there was little to bring back, for all that awaited us were four waggons of wheat, a sugar van and four empty water tanks. By the time the sun glared down from its zenith, all shunting had been completed and, after oiling, fuelling and watering 2611, we were ready to head back by half-past one.

During the return journey, the crew promised to show me engine

No. 2610 and after travelling some two and a half hours, we suddenly stopped on a huge soil embankment built across a thickly wooded valley. As the fireman took a spanner to 2611's motion, I followed the driver some yards, until he indicated a protrusion of maroon metal way down the bank. 'That's her,' he said, 'She's buried there forever now.' One wet night, No. 2610 had been coming back from Mpanda when the heavy rains caused the embankment to collapse. Being dark no one was aware of this and the train plunged into the ravine killing both crew. Despite the obvious difficulties in retrieving the engine, the Mechanical Engineer wished to save 2610, but the Civil Engineer stated that retrieval would be both awkward and costly whilst, left where it had fallen, the engine would provide an excellent foundation upon which to rebuild the track bed! Much argument ensued, but the Civil Engineer, being the senior man, won the day and 2610 was destined to lie in the earth. Even today, the engine is mourned by Tabora's motive power staff, as locomotives are in short supply. A vicious attack by tsetse flies drove us back to our engine and, leaving its hapless sister, 'The Crate' continued on through the woods.

By dusk we reached Ugalla River, the infamous crocodile- and hippo-infested region which often causes the line to be completely closed during the rainy season. For when that river misbehaves, the delicate boulder-strewn bank supporting the railway is destroyed and Mpanda is cut off from the world. By this time I had returned to my coach and leaning out of the window I intrepidly watched our precarious 10 m.p.h. passage over the swamp; wheel flanges grated against the uneven track and I almost imagined I could see the boulders moving under the train's weight! The sun, now reduced to a scarlet ball, coloured the water with brilliant weals of light, broken only by the reedy clusters in the swamp. Our train must have looked gold-plated to the tribal fishermen watching from their frail wooden boats. Leaving the river, I began to prepare my evening meal in the little kitchen; 'The Crate's' exhaust rasped away up front and, once again, we rolled onward into the night.

Space prevents me telling many of the intricacies of that remarkable weekend: I partly rode footplate on that second night, though I confess I slept for most of it. It was well into Sunday morning before 'The Crate' got us back into Tabora yard. Bidding farewell to the crew, I went back to collect my belongings from the coach and, as I did so, 2611 trundled past on her way to the engine shed. A flurry of steam, a whistle, a wave and she was gone, whilst all around me lay the quiet, lifeless goods yard of a Tabora Sunday. My adventure was over.

Watching the engine go, I could have wept tears of anguish, for if anything had ever fulfilled the mysticism of adventure, it had been that weekend. During my experiences with 2611, I had felt those illusive emotions which artists have tried to engender for centuries: after all is not a steam engine as likely to consummate them as anything else? If romanticism has a niche in the human heart, if fairy tales belong with humanity and if adventure inspires the spirit, then I must weep, for in that red engine they had lived for me and, if only transiently, carried me with them to their sublime heights.

E.A.R. Nos.	Builder	Date
2601–2606	Bagnall	1947
2607–2609	Vulcan Foundry, Lancs	1952
2610–2612	Bagnall	1952

Leading Dimensions

Cylinders	$17\frac{1}{2}$ in. $\times$ 23 in.
Boiler pressure	180 lb per sq. in.
Driving wheel diameter	3 ft 7 in.
Grate area	27 sq. ft
Tractive effort 85% b.p.	25,050 lb
Total length	61 ft
Total weight f.w.o.	100 tons
Oil capacity	1,300 gallons
Water capacity	4,200 gallons

LIST OF PLATES AND TEXT REFERENCES